Laura Barnett

Laura Barnett is an arts journalist, theatre critic and features writer for several national newspapers and magazines, including *The Guardian*, *The Observer* and *Time Out London*. She lives in south London with her husband, actor and musician Andrew Glen. She also writes fiction.

ADVICE FROM THE PLAYERS

Laura Barnett

NICK HERN BOOKS

London

www.nickhernbooks.co.uk

A Nick Hern Book

ADVICE FROM THE PLAYERS

First published in Great Britain in 2014
by Nick Hern Books Limited
The Glasshouse, 49a Goldhawk Road, London W12 8QP

Cover image by Getty Images/Peter Dazeley

Designed and typeset by
Nick Hern Books, London
Printed and bound in Great Britain by
Clays Ltd, Bungay, Suffolk

A CIP catalogue record for this book
is available from the British Library

ISBN 978 1 84842 358 9

Contents

Introduction   ix

The Players   xiii

Part One: Learning the Craft

To Train or Not to Train?   2

Acting as a Child or Teenager   7

Applying to Drama School   10

Surviving Drama School   16

Training for Musical Theatre   21

Passionate Amateurs: Finding Other Ways In   24

Some Words of Caution   28

Part Two: Landing the Part

Getting an Agent   34

Confidence: The Magic Ingredient   40

Networking   43

Auditions: A Guide to Success   48

Typecasting – and How to Live with It   67

Learning to Say No   71

Coping with Rejection   76

Part Three: Preparing the Part

Building a Character   82

Lines – and When to Learn Them   94

The Dos and Don'ts of Rehearsal   98

Part Four: Getting It Right

Making Use of Technique   106

Acting for Stage   115

Acting for Camera   120

Acting Comedy   131

Acting Shakespeare   136

Improvising   141

Coping with Stage Fright   144

Staying Sane When Things Go Wrong   150

Going the Distance   156

Part Five: Taking Criticism

Directors: The Good, the So-So, and   160
    the Downright Awful

Reviews: Friend or Foe?   172

'Reputation is Everything': How to Ensure   179
    Yours Stays Good

A Few Words on Fame   187

Part Six: Keeping Going

Day Jobs: How to Make Ends Meet without   192
    Losing Hope

Exercising Body and Mind   196

Surviving the Tough Times   201

Making Time for a Life Beyond Acting   206

Staying Inspired   211

Acknowledgements   218

Introduction

'What advice would you give a young actor?' This is the question I asked a different actor, roughly once a month for seven years, as part of 'Portrait of the Artist', a series of artist interviews I conducted for the *Guardian*.

The actors' answers were diverse, and invariably fascinating. Martin Shaw said it was best not to even try acting unless you have an absolutely burning desire to do it – and to walk away immediately if you are at all attracted by celebrity. Penelope Wilton advised listening to your fellow actors above all other things. 'Acting is a communal thing,' she said. 'You must make sure you don't act in a bubble.' Stephen Mangan's advice was characteristically frank: 'Be on time, work hard, don't be a dick.' And Olivia Williams simply said, with (I suspect) her tongue placed firmly in her cheek: 'Do something else.'

Over the years, I formed the impression of a repository of advice living in the heads of busy professional actors: passed on occasionally to those just entering the profession, in rehearsal rooms, on film sets, or over a few beers in the pub – or, indeed, in newspaper interviews such as mine. As the wife of an actor, too, I knew – and still know – how invaluable this advice could be to the listener: my husband often comes back from rehearsals fired up by the conversations he's had with older actors; carrying their battle-scarred tales of auditioning, touring, working with directors they variously admired or loathed. But generally, this repository seemed an untapped resource: a library, if you like, with no catalogue; no means of accessing the books that line its shelves.

This, then, is what I have tried to do with *Advice from the Players*: place a ladder up to those tall, dusty shelves, and draw down the books that seem most interesting and most useful. Each of the twenty-six actors I have interviewed for this book has kindly, with the honesty and candour that the best actors all seem to share, scoured their minds and memories for the hard-won lessons they have learnt thus far in their careers, and would like to pass on.

They, and I, have every sort of fellow actor in mind as the recipient: from the teenager enjoying her Saturday performing-arts classes, and thinking about applying to drama school; to the twenty-something graduate writing endless unanswered letters to agents; or the seasoned amateur performer in his sixties, looking for tips on how to sharpen up his act.

I have arranged the actors' advice into six chapters, each of which reflects a different aspect of the profession – from training, to keeping going through hard times (of which, as any actor will testify, there may be many). Read the book cover to cover, if you like; or dip in and out whenever you feel like it – to build your confidence before that big audition, perhaps; or while preparing to rehearse a play, and wondering just how much research you should be doing to shape your character.

Some of the advice will be contradictory – every actor's experience of the profession is unique, after all – and you may find you disagree with some of it. But even in disagreeing, you may discover that new light is cast on aspects of your work. For this, ultimately, is the central purpose of this book: to provide guidance and inspiration on every aspect of the actor's complex, fascinating craft. These are not rules to follow slavishly, but slivers of experience – some funny, some practical, many both these things – cut from the varied lives and careers of professionals who know how challenging acting can be. And, of course, how endlessly rewarding.

Laura Barnett

The Players

Jane Asher	Paul McGann
Zawe Ashton	Bill Paterson
Helen Baxendale	Jenna Russell
Tracie Bennett	Simon Russell Beale
Jo Brand	Antony Sher
Simon Callow	Samantha Spiro
Brian Cox	Imogen Stubbs
Oliver Ford Davies	David Thaxton
Mark Gatiss	Luke Treadaway
David Harewood	Mark Umbers
Lenny Henry	Harriet Walter
Mathew Horne	Julie Walters
Lesley Manville	Samuel West

LEARNING
THE CRAFT

To Train
or Not to Train?

Three years at drama school, a university degree followed by a postgraduate acting course – or relying on raw talent and accumulated experience? There are many routes into acting: here, our Players reflect on the paths they themselves took, and weigh up the pros and cons of training.

You don't have to be a trained actor, or have been in the business for many years, to be any good. That's nonsense, patently: you can get someone off the street who can be stunning. Some actors are very snobbish about this, and feel that it shouldn't be so. It may be annoying, but it's true. **Jane Asher**

Training gives you the chance to play roles that you will probably never be cast as, and to act without the pressure of real audiences and critics. You're students, so you're forgiven. You can have a go at finding out what it is that you actually like doing. **Julie Walters**

I never had much training. I learned on the job. Keep your eyes and ears open: everyone's always got something you can learn from. Put it in the box to bring out another time. In our game, there is no right way or wrong way. **Jenna Russell**

Training is incredibly important. I didn't go to drama school because I started off life as an academic; it wasn't until I started working as a lecturer at Edinburgh University that I thought, 'Actually, this isn't what I want to do with my life.' But by that time I was twenty-seven, and I thought it was too late for drama school. I missed out on many things by not training. As the decades passed, this has probably corrected itself. At least, I hope it has. **Oliver Ford Davies**

I always had a certain facility for acting. If I'd become an actor straight away without going to drama school, I would have just emphasised that facility over and over again. I think I would have been the most hollow and shallow actor that existed. But that's just me: others get on very well without formal training. **Simon Callow**

Everybody should do drama training – even scientists. It's about learning how you deal with yourself: about meeting yourself, in terms of your voice, your movement, your imagination, your thinking. It's physical, it's spiritual, it's mental, it's emotional. It's every aspect of a human being under scrutiny. The better the school, the more that's taken care of. **Brian Cox**

There's no bar to success in this game.

It doesn't matter where you're from;
it doesn't matter whether you're
fifteen or thirty-five.

I'm a comprehensive-school boy from
Small Heath in Birmingham:

I'd only read three plays when I
turned up at RADA.

None of that matters.

The business needs fresh faces, fresh
energy. You learn on the job, and you
never stop learning.

David Harewood

Going to drama school is particularly important if you're not from London, and you don't know anybody in the business: it gives you a chance to get an agent. That's what happened to me. I had no belief that I would actually ever get paid for acting. I remember being amazed when I actually got a paid job. In fact, I'm still amazed every time it happens. **Helen Baxendale**

Acting is not just about being an actor: it's also about understanding your place in the world. What drama means, what writers do; the dangers of fashion; what's popular but isn't necessarily good. Through training, you learn to purify and rarefy and boil all this down to something quite essential. **Brian Cox**

Go with your gut about whether drama school is for you. I'm from quite a working-class family. We didn't have much money, and when a London drama school offered me a scholarship and I turned it down, they called three or four times offering me more and more money. But something in my heart said, 'No, this is not for you: you are learning as you go.' I continued as a stand-up – and I don't regret that one bit. **Mathew Horne**

There are people who haven't been to drama school and are great actors and have done very well. But I also know some so-called great actors who could have gone to drama school and learnt a lot. **Brian Cox**

My regret is that I never went to drama school – I started so young. To learn technique at drama school is very, very useful – I had to pick it up in bits along the way, from directors or voice coaches. You do pick it up over time, but I'd have liked to have it all officially, much earlier. **Jane Asher**

People who haven't trained actually tend to be much more technically conscious than actors who have. A proper training, you see, is really about a technique of the emotions, rather than a technique of skills. Actors like Ian McKellen and Derek Jacobi haven't trained, as such – they just learned on the hoof by observing other people. **Simon Callow**

Acting as a Child
or Teenager

Are those weekend drama classes worth it? Should you apply to join the National Youth Theatre? And what are the potential costs of becoming a child star? The Players who also started young share their wisdom.

If you're starting out as a child actor, as I did, don't take it too seriously. It's important not to get too intense about the whole business of acting. Once you're in the rehearsal room with the director you've got to take it deeply seriously, of course – but when you come outside, try to keep it in perspective. **Jane Asher**

I have a horror of six-year-old children going to full-time stage school. I think it's wrong. When you're little, theatre should be fun. Send children to drama groups instead. They give young children confidence; there's no pressure. **Jenna Russell**

You know if you want to do it or you don't: you're massive on am–dram, and a big musical-theatre geek, or you're not. So if it's something you want to do, do as much performing as possible. I was a geek until I was about thirteen: then I got into girls and Radiohead. I still did all the am–dram and performing, but I stopped being madly intense about it. **David Thaxton**

Drama groups are a great idea for young children with excess energy. I was five when I started at Anna Scher. I instantly connected with it. I walked in and saw a row of laundry baskets arranged on a stage: one marked 'masks', one marked 'wigs', one marked 'props'. I remember going, 'Yeah, I'm going to like this.' I ended up staying for fourteen years. **Zawe Ashton**

I strongly recommend auditioning for the National Youth Theatre. It was a very useful place to find out about drama school: I met a lot of people there who were a year ahead of me in the system, and already auditioning. I remember sitting in the halls of residence, writing down a list of the five drama schools that everybody seemed to keep talking about. Then when it came to auditioning, I was able to stay with people I'd met at NYT, all round the country. **Luke Treadaway**

Audition for the National Youth Theatre. I went when I was sixteen. The process of auditioning, and then of doing a four-week summer school with like-minded people from all over the country, was intense. It was probably the first time I'd met other people in the same gene pool who really wanted to act for a living. It can be intimidating – but you'll learn a hell of a lot. **Zawe Ashton**

As far as acting in childhood goes, I'd say: don't.

I'm lucky that I survived it. Both my parents loved all of us desperately, and I wanted to do it. But I have memories of being away from home at a very young age, and being homesick. Going up for an audition against loads of other children is very difficult: children will come up against enough knocks without having to put themselves up to be knocked down. Then there's the terrible business of whether you can break through into adult roles. You see so many big child stars who do end up rather messed up.

Jane Asher

Applying to Drama School

There are currently eighteen accredited drama schools in the UK, and countless other acting courses are springing up offering everything from month-long workshops to post-graduate degrees. At the most prestigious schools, thousands of young actors are often competing for every place. Here, our Players guide you through the maze that is choosing a drama school, and give the inside track on standing out from the crowd.

Aim high. Apply to the best-known schools, as they will usually attract the best teachers. If you're lucky enough to have a choice of places on offer, go for the one where you feel you can most easily talk to the auditioning panel: the place that feels like it 'gets' you. **Harriet Walter**

It's awful that you can't
get grants to go to drama
school any more:
it's going to be a profession full
of middle-class people.

I know it's expensive:
if it was me now going into
drama school, I wouldn't be
able to go.

But please still do it, whatever
your background. We need you.

Julie Walters

**Start with the best
drama schools,
and brace yourself:**
there's an awful lot of people
trying to get in. I was very
abruptly, and rather cruelly,
turned down by the two top
schools.

It's a good lesson for the life of
an actor, really:
**you will always be
competing for parts
against the odds.**

Antony Sher

Do your research before you go to drama school – and don't be swayed by your teachers. Mine dissuaded from me going to drama school in favour of an academic degree: I only just realised the mistake in time, and managed to change my course at the last minute. Take all the advice you can – but don't let anyone put you off by telling you that acting is going to be hard. Of course it is: that's not a reason not to try. **Zawe Ashton**

There are a few unknowns in an audition, and it's up to the actor to make them as few as possible. If you're doing audition pieces for drama school, then you should have chosen pieces that you can't wait to do; that you're good casting for; that you know terribly well; and that you do terribly well. If none of these things is true for you, choose another piece. **Samuel West**

Most of the accredited drama schools offer a good training. What really counts is the contacts the school has, and how they can propel you into the business. After a three-year course, you really do need to know what the prospects are of getting an agent and a job. It might sound quite Machiavellian, but it's very important. **Samantha Spiro**

A one-year course is a better option for a lot of people than a three-year degree. The whole point of it is to get an agent anyway, so if you've got a one-year course that you know good agents will come to at the end, just go with that. **David Thaxton**

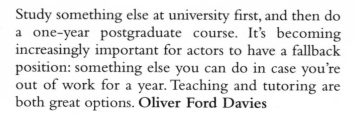

Study something else at university first, and then do a one-year postgraduate course. It's becoming increasingly important for actors to have a fallback position: something else you can do in case you're out of work for a year. Teaching and tutoring are both great options. **Oliver Ford Davies**

Don't ever be deterred because of your background. We got the best of times in the fifties and sixties: doors were opening rather than closing. I was actually given a grant to go to drama school. It wasn't huge; perhaps £250 – but in those days, that was enough to live on. **Bill Paterson**

If you have a sense of the theatre as a vocation, and as a very significant job – as it might be if you were a doctor or an engineer; that you absolutely have a massive contribution to make to society, and it is vital that what you do is as right and challenging and brave as could be – then you should try to find a drama school that suits you. **Simon Callow**

Make sure the college has a very rigorous television course. The industry's changing, and your training needs to reflect all aspects of the business – not just stage, but film, TV and radio. **David Harewood**

Your training should set you up for everything. Nowadays, you need to do a fair amount of TV and camera work at drama school as well as theatre. We only had one weekend on that in three years, which now seems ludicrous. At that time, there was an old-fashioned opinion that we would go into the classical theatre and have a career based solely on that. That model isn't relevant any more. You will want to spend a lot of your career doing telly. **Samantha Spiro**

Start with the accredited schools. There are some new schools that aren't yet accredited, but there are many more that never will be. We're training too many people, and some of them in the wrong way. Some of the teaching is very good, but some of it seems to fit the actor to the profession, rather than the other way round. **Samuel West**

Don't just choose the best drama school: pick the place you feel most comfortable in. I ended up at RADA by accident, and I was very lucky. But some people I know went to schools they didn't particularly enjoy. Some students are much happier with a more physical training; others with musical theatre. So think hard about the kind of training you want to do, and where you want to do it. **David Harewood**

Read the prospectuses carefully. When I read RADA's, it seemed like a holiday camp. And when I read Drama Centre's, it sounded like a concentration camp. I thought, 'That's what I need: an acting boot camp.' And that's very much what I got. **Simon Callow**

Surviving
Drama School

You've chosen a school, you've secured your place. Now the real work must begin – and seriously tough it can turn out to be. Let the Players inspire you to get the best out of your training.

Start from a humble point of view about your own knowledge. Be open to everything. It's better to risk being a prat at drama school than in the outside world. **Harriet Walter**

Maintain your own identity. It's very easy to go into drama college and come out a decent singer and dancer, but look the same as everyone else. That's boring. Know what you're good at: find your niche, and do it really well. And go easy on the fake tan. **David Thaxton**

Remember, throughout your time at drama school, that you're there for a reason: you love acting, and you're good at it. They wouldn't have let you in otherwise. Some people start feeling, within a couple of weeks, that they're an absolute fraud. But what drama school is ultimately doing is giving you tools for your toolbox. You might not use any of these techniques for a few years, but your vocabulary will be hugely enriched. **Luke Treadaway**

It's impossible entirely to get rid of self-consciousness as an actor, but a good drama school – and one you work hard at – should free you from it to a large extent, so that you feel you are emboldened to make brave decisions (and fail at them if necessary). At drama school, you're not worried about what the casting director who's in tonight thinks of this decision; what your agent thinks; whether this is going to go down well with the TV executives. All those things make actors less good. Drama school is a very good place not to have to ask yourself those questions. **Samuel West**

The things I learnt at drama school are things I still employ to this day, almost fifty years later. It's only as I get older that I think, 'Oh, I see, *that's* what it meant.' It was one of the most exciting experiences of my life, and formative in every aspect. It gave me in-roads to everything. **Brian Cox**

I didn't think having fun was part of being at drama school at all. We were very subversive – this was the late sixties and early seventies – but always within the framework of believing that acting was a very important thing. You could compare it to joining the SAS, or becoming part of a religious order. There was that sense that we were being trained up for something incredibly demanding, and incredibly important. **Simon Callow**

The two most important things you get from drama school are fitness – emotional, physical, vocal – and the invaluable experience of making a complete tit of yourself in front of people who don't care. You can't really get that anywhere else. **Samuel West**

When at drama school, don't waste time inventing excuses for not trying or really exploring things, even if they seem uncool or embarrassing or beneath you. Go for it all. Strip away the superfluous fronts that will only make your acting a shallow imitation of other people's acting. **Harriet Walter**

Drama school can be intimidating. You might get there aged eighteen, and be studying alongside people who are twenty-three and have already done loads of plays. To begin with, it might feel like all these people have amazing ideas. You just have to work hard, keep your head down, and realise that drama school is very different to university. I had a lot of friends who'd gone to university and had a few hours of lectures a week: we had classes from 9 a.m. till 9 p.m. It's all-consuming. **Luke Treadaway**

Try to go deep into the meaning of a part and a play and draw things from an honest part of you deep inside. You may not get many chances to do this under pressure in the real world. You will look like less of a prat if you go for something sincerely and fail, than if you resist and stand on the edge smirking. But (and this is the balancing act) protect your ego from teachers that you sense are stripping you down out of some kind of power trip, rather than helping you reveal your most honest work. **Harriet Walter**

Don't be afraid of taking risks while you're young. Steve [Pemberton, with whom Gatiss, Jeremy Dyson and Reece Shearsmith created the League of Gentlemen] and I devised a show in 1988 called *Damage Your Children*. It was a game-show spoof in which a child was tortured to death. We took it to the National Student Drama Festival and it caused a bit of a stink. But it was tremendous fun. I wouldn't do something like that now, but that's the kind of thing you should be doing at that age. **Mark Gatiss**

Acting is not therapy. Be very sure that if the drama school does a lot of work on your personality – if it's going to take you apart – that it puts you back together again afterwards. **Samuel West**

Resist being force-fed technique. I didn't train, but I've known a lot of actors who were extraordinary and individual before they went to drama school, and came out of that process as a homogenised type of actor. There are other people for whom the reverse is true. But for me, training is more about constantly learning from other people. You're only as good as who you're acting opposite. **Mark Umbers**

Eat well, keep healthy, and know that you're there to work. You'll have lots of time to pick up on the socialising when you leave. **Luke Treadaway**

The important thing about training

is that it buys you space – three years, ideally –

in which to make an absolute and total berk of yourself,

in front of your fellow actors, who are going through the same thing.

It's a controlled environment in which you can

unpack your own neuroses, your inhibitions,

your resistances. And if it's a well-devised course, you can slowly – having, as it were disassembled yourself – reach back towards the light.

Simon Callow

Training for Musical Theatre

Musical-theatre performers must, for the most part, be great all-rounders, able to dance and sing as well as act – and with the stamina to survive eight high-energy shows a week. Jenna Russell and David Thaxton, both of whom have won Olivier awards for their work in musicals, offer their tips on training for success.

Be wary of too many singing lessons. If you are with the wrong teacher, you can end up losing your individual sound. But it's always good to keep warmed up: if you've got an audition, do a good warm-up, and ask someone to go through the music with you. **Jenna Russell**

Choose your singing teacher very carefully. I heard some horror stories when I was at college. One guy was known as the Butcher of the North: he was ruining all these young singers' voices in Manchester. If you don't have a good connection with someone, move on. **David Thaxton**

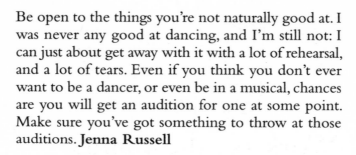

Be open to the things you're not naturally good at. I was never any good at dancing, and I'm still not: I can just about get away with it with a lot of rehearsal, and a lot of tears. Even if you think you don't ever want to be a dancer, or even be in a musical, chances are you will get an audition for one at some point. Make sure you've got something to throw at those auditions. **Jenna Russell**

Don't smoke. Countless people do, of course. I did vocal studies at college – classical singing and opera – and I remember being given this huge list of things that you weren't allowed to eat or do to look after your voice. No dairy, no alcohol. I remember thinking, 'Bollocks to that.' There are no set rules: you have to find what works for you. I can handle late nights, I can handle drinking and all the rest, but I can't do shouting at people in nightclubs. **David Thaxton**

Work on the things that don't come naturally to you.

The ability to move well is really important: if you're not a good mover, work on it. Do dance classes. But that said, I myself can't dance and I don't care. It makes me feel sick.

David Thaxton

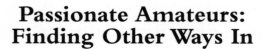

Passionate Amateurs:
Finding Other Ways In

Acting means many different things to different people. For the thousands of people around the country who participate in amateur theatre, it's an opportunity to unwind, have fun and make friends. And the chance to turn professional may be just around the corner, too – as it was for Bill Paterson, who first acted in amateur productions. Many stand-up comedians have also made the leap into 'straight' acting without formal training. Here, our Players offer their advice on how to get the best out of acting as an amateur, and reflect on some of the less conventional routes into the profession.

Consider stand-up as a route into acting. Comics, on the whole, make very good actors. Just look at all the comics who've gone on to do film and serious acting: Billy Connolly, Victoria Wood, Eddie Izzard, Steve Coogan. But you must try to establish yourself as a decent comic first – don't just do it for a couple of years and then think, 'Now I can go on tour with the Royal Shakespeare Company.' That's not going to happen: you need to get good at one thing before you try the next. **Jo Brand**

There's no point in anybody saying, grandly, that everybody has to have a training, or that anybody who came out of the amateur-theatre movement is not going to be a good actor. **I know many wonderful actors who came out of amateur theatre,** and others should be continuously encouraged to do so. It's a house of many mansions.

Simon Callow

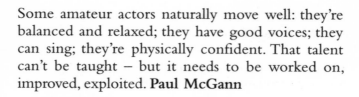

Some amateur actors naturally move well: they're balanced and relaxed; they have good voices; they can sing; they're physically confident. That talent can't be taught – but it needs to be worked on, improved, exploited. **Paul McGann**

Learn from your mistakes. You don't have to go to drama school to do that – you can do it at university, or from doing plays in an amateur setting. **Helen Baxendale**

The average amateur actor – especially a man of a certain age – is welcomed into a company by people saying, 'We're delighted you're here: we need men of your age.' Showbusiness doesn't work that way. There's lots of men my age going up for the same jobs. Nobody gets excited because you're sixty-five. **Bill Paterson**

The biggest challenge for amateur actors is not to let it all get too cosy. They can seem too pleased with each other, and with what they do. The most important thing for any amateur group is to get a really tough director. **Simon Callow**

Don't be afraid to take an unorthodox route into acting. I'm not a trained actor: I did a drama and film studies degree in Manchester, which I chose purely on the basis of the city. It was a very academic course, with no performance training – all the performance had to be done extracurricular to the course. But I don't feel like it's held me back in any way. **Mathew Horne**

Do as many plays as you can while at university. If you're passionate about it, you'll find the time. University is a great place to act. You don't have what I imagine would be the pressure of a drama school: there's no sense of competition, no passing-out parade at the end where people get agents and meet casting directors. You can just get on with enjoying the work. **Mark Umbers**

Go with the flow. I really only became an actor by accident, after drifting into a semi-professional, semi-amateur theatre group in Glasgow. I'd been in the building trade for years, as a quantity surveyor, but I was hopeless at it. I discovered there was a teaching course at the Royal Scottish Academy of Music and Drama, so I signed up for that, and it coincided with the start-up of a theatre-in-education company. I joined that, thinking, 'I'll try acting for a few months.' All these years later, I'm still doing it. **Bill Paterson**

Some Words of Caution

Acting professionally isn't for the faint-hearted: it's a career full of tension, near-misses and sleepless nights, not to mention the potential weeks, months – or even years – you might spend out of work. Here, our Players offer a few clear-sighted words of warning to those determined to dedicate their lives to acting.

Don't do it. Acting is heartbreaking, humiliating, crushing – and the chances of getting work are very remote. Of course someone who is really, truly determined won't be put off by any of this. But it's a good way of weeding people out. **Jane Asher**

Take a pessimistic look at your chances of getting work. At any one time, almost ninety per cent of actors aren't working. You have to be prepared to live a hand-to-mouth existence; to take work that you don't really want to do; or to spend months going round in a van, performing to a group of moody teenagers for £2. Only a tiny minority of actors actually get through to the good, well-paid jobs. If you want it enough, you'll be prepared to put up with all the crap – but you need to accept that it's going to be really hard. **Jo Brand**

Be honest with yourself.

Ask yourself, 'Can I possibly be stopped?' If you're going into acting on a whim, or for spurious reasons –

> because you want to be famous, or you think there might be money in it –

then **just turn around**. You'll just get a kicking. Only the people that can't possibly be dissuaded from acting should be doing it.

> That's almost the minimum requirement.

Paul McGann

Don't do it. There's no jobs. **Mathew Horne**

Ask yourself, 'Must I do this?', and be damn sure that the answer is yes. It's a question stolen from Rilke's advice to a young poet. The poet sends his verse to Rilke saying, 'Are these any good?' And Rilke says, 'That's not the question – the question is, must I write?' If the answer to that is 'yes', you're fine. It's useful to know that you've got talent. But talent is a funny thing: it doesn't always make itself known very early on, and not always in a way that is useful. **Samuel West**

If there's something else in life you love as much as acting, go and do that. If there's nothing else, then obviously you have to do this. The highs are incredible: when it goes your way, there's nothing like it. But it can be horrible. You can be out of work for years at a time; you can have a year with no work and two auditions and not get either of them. There are incredibly fortunate actors who just don't stop working, but that's not something you can really aspire to be: it only happens to a precious few. **David Thaxton**

Be realistic. I think if the work had dried up for me, I'd have done something else. I would not have hung by the phone for years on end. My ego couldn't have stood it. **Julie Walters**

Give yourself a certain number of years. After that, if it's not working out, you might want to make a brave decision and change professions. I know actors who've spent a lifetime out of work, and who get very disappointed and very bitter. But, from the outside, you want to say, 'Listen, you're not getting work. This isn't going to work for you, this horribly tough profession. You would do yourself a favour if you did something else.' That said, when I auditioned for RADA in 1968, they sent me a letter saying, 'We urge you to think about doing a different profession: this is not for you.' And they were wrong. You've got to know in yourself whether it's for you or it's not. **Antony Sher**

LANDING
THE PART

Getting an Agent

The number of professional actors has grown hugely over the past few decades: Spotlight, the actors' directory, has multiplied from two slim volumes, in its early days, to ten. So it's no surprise that the number of agencies has grown, too. Hundreds of theatrical agents are now operating in the UK, and the best ones are hugely oversubscribed. So how do you sort a good agent from a bad one, and then persuade them to represent you? And can you succeed in acting without an agent to chivvy things along?

Not to have an agent is a very, very difficult thing. My agent has been my pal for thirty years. Drama schools should be able to help you with getting one for yourself – but if you're still looking, don't be frightened of bombarding agents. Most of them are very generous and responsive; they expect to be bothered. Bombard them until they're prepared to see you. Just keep trying: there's no magic trick. **Simon Russell Beale**

A good agent is worth their weight in gold.

They have a bit of **vision**, a bit of **foresight**: they can see where their client should go.

That's even more necessary now than it ever was: the profession is much more chaotic, and the failure rate is much higher. Together, you and your agent have got to be the arbiters of what you do.

Brian Cox

Look carefully at an agent's list. I got my agent though Catherine Tate: I did a show in Edinburgh, which Catherine had seen, and her agent took me on. She's unusual in the industry in that she has very few clients, and they include people like Ardal O'Hanlon, Simon Pegg and Catherine Tate: all sorts of writer-performer types. She had helped build up all these big stars. I thought maybe, if I stuck with her, she could do the same for me. **Mathew Horne**

Use your instinct to choose an agent. If you've got three of the top agents coming after you, pick the one you get on with best: they're all going to have the same sorts of scripts coming in. But for some people, it's a result just to get any sort of representation: so, unless it's some random agency off the internet, just go with whoever you can get. **Luke Treadaway**

Don't feel obligated to go with an agent because they're a big name. It's not a good start to the relationship if they make you feel insecure, and as though you should be very grateful. Go with somebody who wants you and understands you. There should be equality between you. **Samantha Spiro**

Keep letters to agents short and professional. Some people in my year at drama school put jokes in their letters, or went for a very personal approach. Having been on the receiving end of that, casting my own plays, I can tell you that it just doesn't work. Agents will be looking at your photo; your

CV; your drama school; the role you're in, and whether they can come and see you perform: nothing else. **Zawe Ashton**

Cold-calling an agent with nothing to offer isn't a good idea. Try to get into a fringe show: in those first few years, being paid is almost a bonus. It's much better to have something to invite an agent along to. **Samantha Spiro**

Trust your agent. Don't keep ringing them. If there's nothing in for you, there's nothing in. **Tracie Bennett**

Make sure that you're being represented by your agent in the way you want to be, and that they understand the range of acting that you are aiming to do. I've ended up doing a lot of telly, when actually I really like doing theatre. I assumed I was never being offered anything in the theatre, but actually it was a choice that my old agency was making: they were telling me about the telly and film instead of the theatre. **Imogen Stubbs**

Remember that your agent works for you. You hire them for their service, not the other way around. It is easy to be intimidated by one's agent and view them as the hostile gatekeeper to the jobs out there. This is a paranoid delusion, of course – but not miles from the truth as it affects the actor out there in the tough cold world. **Harriet Walter**

The more you do, and the more you show you can do it, the better your relationship with your agent will be. I don't know whether being their mate is a good thing. **Helen Baxendale**

When I was starting out, there was a whole different feeling about agents and what they did. A really good agent understood that he had a client that was going to develop. He would bring on a young actor and place him in a theatre, and say, 'Take this young actor', and the relationship would pay off. As a result, I was with my first agent for nineteen years; and I've been with my second for nearly thirty years. The structure is so different now, and it's much harder for young actors. They're also at the mercy of so many other elements: glamour, personality, and this horrible thing called celebrity. **Brian Cox**

Look at what's on paper at the end of the year. If there haven't been any meetings, and your income is nothing, then you have to think about finding other people to represent you. But it's a Catch-22: if you get rid of an agent, you have to find another one, and that's pretty hard if you're not in anything. So if you want to move agents, you have to bite the bullet while you're in something that you're really good in, and move as quickly as possible. **Mark Umbers**

You know it's time to leave an agent when you realise they take no joy in your triumphs, and have no pity in your failures. Don't sign with somebody who patronises you, or makes you feel you ought to be grateful that they're making a phone call on your behalf. A small agency can be much better: you're moving forward together. **Imogen Stubbs**

Confidence:
The Magic Ingredient

Auditioning, screen-testing, turning up on the first day of rehearsals to face a room of blank stares – not to mention stepping out on stage on opening night… Every stage of the acting process requires confidence – or at least the appearance of it. Here's how to keep a tight grip on that core – and sometimes elusive – self-belief.

Succeeding in auditions is all about believing in yourself. I had a mad, insane belief in myself when I first came into the business. I felt I had something unique: I thought, 'Well, if you don't want me, you're not worth working with.' That's the attitude you've got to go in with. If you believe you have a unique talent, you have, basically: unless you're completely potty. And even then, if you believe it, it's there. **Julie Walters**

Confidence is the bottom line.

> The business of acting is actually relatively simple – anybody could do it.

The business of making a living as an actor is the difficult part.

> Being able to keep your head above water requires a type of operation that is beyond the work itself.

Bill Paterson

Be honest about what you can do. If you really think you're right for the part, and you've got an agent, then say to them, 'Look, I really want to be seen for this.' But when you say that, you'd better be sure you've read the play, know the part, know the theatre, and might actually be what they're looking for. Conversely, if you get seen for something and you haven't got a chance in hell, don't sweat it: just enjoy the audition. **Samuel West**

Relaxation is the nub of it. You can't be good unless you're relaxed. It's about confidence, and it can disappear so easily, no matter how much work you've done. Actors are so vulnerable. You need to be confident enough to be truly relaxed and open. It's a delicate thing. **Helen Baxendale**

I do wish, in some ways, that I had trained. I think it would have given me an extra jolt of confidence that I still feel I lack. I am sometimes my own worst critic: I think a lot of actors are. But that can also be a good thing: it's never good to be too confident. **Mark Umbers**

Nerves set in when you're not feeling confident. So how do you get more confident? By being sure of your lines. By knowing who your character is. By working on the moments that don't feel comfortable: asking the director questions; running those moments with the other actors. By warming yourself up physically and vocally. If you've got all those things in place, there's no reason to feel nervous. **Samantha Spiro**

Networking

It's not what you know, but who you know... Well, not always — but building relationships with directors, writers, producers and fellow performers could just further your career. So how do you do that without seeming pushy? Should you write to directors you admire — and if so, what should you say? And is there any hope for the natural introvert, for whom the very idea of attending that first-night party is enough to bring them out in hives?

Only write to a director if you really feel compelled to do it. Years ago, I went up for an audition for Rufus Norris, for *Cabaret*. I didn't get the job, but I thought he was so extraordinary in what he was doing, and his approach to it, that I felt compelled to write to him and just say, 'I really, really enjoyed working on the material with you. Obviously you're quite extraordinary, and I hope one day we get to work together.' We never have, but I still hope one day we do. **Jenna Russell**

My partner [the director] Greg Doran often says I should network more. That's not my talent. Whatever talent I have is for the stage, not for chatting at cocktail parties. **Antony Sher**

Build relationships with people who actually like what you do.

Developing a shorthand with another actor, writer or director doesn't come along all the time: it's taken me about twenty years in the business to build up about five such people.

Nurture these people, keep them close. They're your muses.

Zawe Ashton

Write to directors and writers you admire. When I was young, I was always writing to people and sending out my photograph. It happens much less now – but some directors really do take the time to respond. Be honest, don't be pushy, and above all, be brief. **Lesley Manville**

Pitch letters to directors correctly. Imagine I'm planning a production of *Hamlet*, and I get a letter from an actor who says, 'Dear Sam, I understand you're planning a production of *Hamlet*: I think I'm the prince you're looking for.' You're not: you're an idiot. I don't put on *Hamlet* without knowing who's going to play the main role. So choose your battles. You'll have more luck if you write to me suggesting yourself for a small part for which you're perfectly cast. The most useful folder any director has – and it's not often very fat – is the one marked 'Good and Humble'. **Samuel West**

Go to other shows: you never know who you might meet that might lead to the next job, and you will be keeping up with what's going on in your profession. At the beginning of an acting career, it's important to be open to anything: you can narrow it all down later. **Harriet Walter**

Find yourself some mentors. I've had several. I'd do summer seasons in Blackpool and Great Yarmouth and places like that, and watch the comedians Don Maclean and Nicky Martin do their thing every night. Twelve times a week, these guys would never fail to get laughs. It made me learn that a comedian must never drop below their median level: above that level is true art. **Lenny Henry**

Cultivate relationships. Until people start to say, 'I want to work with you', you've got to keep things going yourself. It's like gardening. Follow things up; write a card to a director you've worked with to say thank you. It sounds a bit contrived, but it works. You don't have to send them champagne. But if you just drop them a little card saying it was a pleasure to work with them, they will remember you – and they'll hopefully work with you again. **Mark Gatiss**

Get into fringe theatre, even if you're not being paid. The rep system that we had in my day no longer exists, but there's a big wave of these fringe pubs doing great, interesting work. It's important to take risks. Not many people risk anything any more – producers or actors – but I've always kept that element of risk. I don't care if I'm rubbish in something. I'm learning all the time. **Tracie Bennett**

Be prepared to share your contacts. When I came back to theatre after a long gap to do a play at the National, it was lovely to see all the young actors sharing their contacts. We had a list up, and every time someone in the cast had someone they knew – a director, or some other famous person – coming to see the show, we'd put their name down on the list. I suppose, when the chips are down, you might be sorry you've told other people: you might end up being rivals. But it's still better to take a sharing, collaborative approach. **Bill Paterson**

Think of someone else's career path that you would like to emulate (but never imitate: you can't) and tell your agent. Then you can ask them to try putting you in touch with the right people to further those aims. It's hard for an actor on the ground to know who the key people are out there in the studios and rehearsal rooms. **Harriet Walter**

You can't force the situation of being in the right place at the right time. I've seen people over the years who are particularly good at networking, but I don't know whether it makes you happier or more employable. I always think it feels a bit false. If you do get on well with a particular director, there's no reason not to drop them an email telling them what you're up to. But only do it if it feels honest, right and real. **Samantha Spiro**

I was advised to change my surname because no one could pronounce it. People still can't pronounce it. But I thought my dad would kill me if I changed it. In the end, I decided that what you need to do is what we can now officially call 'Cumberbatch' it: make sure that you become sufficiently well-known that no one could possibly mispronounce your name. **Mark Gatiss**

Auditions:
A Guide to Success

Ah, the audition – a relaxed, enjoyable opportunity to meet new people, talk about a play, film or TV show, show them how perfect you are for the part… Well, maybe, in an ideal world – but every actor knows how tense and soul-destroying a bad audition can be. So how do you make sure it's a good one? What should you wear? Should you learn your lines, or just have a working knowledge of the play? And how friendly is too friendly? Our Players offer a step-by-step guide to sailing through that audition and – most importantly – ensuring you land that part.

1. Preparing

Find something unusual to read. I haven't auditioned since I was very young, but back when I was auditioning, there's no way I would have done Juliet, or any of the common speeches. I would find something very unusual: a rare or strange poem; anything that would shock them into thinking, 'Oh God, who's this? This is refreshing.' I remember auditioning years ago for *Evita*, the very first time it was being done. I went to meet Hal Prince, the

Broadway director, and sang all my answers to his questions. He thought it was hilarious. **Julie Walters**

Research the script more than the project. In the end, it doesn't matter if you don't know who the director is – it's good if you do, but what they want to see is that you can play that part the best. **Helen Baxendale**

For a theatre audition, read the play as much as you can, and go in armed to discuss the backstory. Read up on the writer and any past productions of the play. Have an angle on the character – not for the sake of being clever, but to understand what *you* would do if you played the part. **Samantha Spiro**

Don't be lazy. Directors, producers and casting directors like to see that you've put some time in: that if you've been given the whole script, you've read it; and that you've got something to say about it. They may not agree with all your thoughts and feelings about the project, but it shows that you're intelligent, and that you're able to read and analyse a script. **Lesley Manville**

Always ask to read the
whole script,
    even if you've only
    been asked to
    prepare one scene.

It's not overkeen:
    it shows you want to
    know anything
    about the character
    that might be useful.

Samuel West

Do your research about the project you're going up for. In my early twenties, I had to audition for a pantomime. I didn't know anything about musicals, so I got a big bumper book of musical songs, and taught myself a song, which I thought was rather pretty. It was 'Tomorrow' from *Annie* – which of course is sung by a little girl. I had absolutely no idea. It was completely inappropriate; they thought I was bonkers. Of course I didn't get the part.
Simon Russell Beale

Be prepared. The worst auditions I've done have been through lack of preparation: just turning up and making stupid choices. I went to an *Avenue Q* audition in my lunch break from working in a bar, wearing smart trousers and a shirt, feeling really silly. If you're prepared, you can still have a bad audition: but then it's just one of those things.
David Thaxton

2. Learning Your Lines

Know your speeches upside down and back to front so that you can respond quickly to whatever the auditioner throws at you. For the same reason, although it is good to have thought through your speeches in great detail and know what you want to say with them, it's also important to be flexible. The auditioner may ask you to do the speech in a completely different way. Even if you disagree, they are probably just looking to see how well you respond to direction. Most people would rather see imperfect potential, and a responsive actor, than someone who is unchanging and rigid – even if they are brilliant. **Harriet Walter**

Don't worry about learning all your lines for an audition. Familiarise yourself with it as much as you can, so you can get eye contact. But if you try to learn it, all you'll be doing is trying to remember the words. **Jenna Russell**

It is worth learning the stuff they send you. We're all so arrogant in Britain that we turn up, look at the bit of paper, and tend to read it very badly. In America, they learn the stuff, and they get their acting coach to work on it with them. The world's changing, and British actors probably need to change with it. **Imogen Stubbs**

Know the audition speech you're given. It didn't used to be that you needed to learn it – you used to just read it. But now you have to know it so well that you can do whatever they want with it in the audition. **Helen Baxendale**

3. Dressing to Kill

A maxi skirt is a great addition to your wardrobe. I always wear one to an audition for a classical play. If I rock up in jeans, it makes me feel less like the part. **Samantha Spiro**

You hear some crazy stuff that certain drama colleges are telling their students: that they've got to wear all black, or the girls have to tart themselves up. The best thing is to approach the audition as yourself, but make it so they can see you in the show without too much difficulty. Think, 'What would the character I'm auditioning for wear now?' **David Thaxton**

Be yourself. I don't approve of all this dressing up to look like the part. A really good director doesn't care what the actor looks like in real life: they know that, whatever you're wearing, you can play characters that are nothing like yourself. **Lesley Manville**

With a screen audition, it's important that you look right for the part. I usually pick a look that is somehow related to the part – though not a slavish imitation. But in the USA, I am told, it is expected of actors to attempt a full costume and make-up – the idea being that casting people have little imagination, and you have to give them a lot of help. **Harriet Walter**

Wear something that makes you feel powerful.

If you're going up for a period drama and you feel like you should wear a ruff, but that doesn't make you feel good – don't do it. But I once went up for a role in a Greek mythical film wearing a full-length one-shouldered Grecian dress with a rope belt. I got the part.

Zawe Ashton

Give a nod to the type of character you're playing with your clothes – but don't go along in costume. I try to look at least as if I'm together and clean. It's tricky, as a woman: so many of the parts you go up for just say 'gorgeous', and you think, 'Well, that's me out, then.' In the end, you can only be yourself. Just be good at what you're doing, and look presentable. **Helen Baxendale**

Screen tests are a hard one. You don't know how far to go with the look. I went up for a telly part cringing about what I was wearing – I could hardly even catch eyes with the producer. But I suppose I looked the part when they went to look back at the film, because I got the job – and that's ultimately what matters. It's an eternally difficult thing, and I don't think I've quite cracked it. Sometimes it works out; sometimes you just feel like a bit of a twit. **Samantha Spiro**

4. Making a Good Impression

Turn up on time. **Lesley Manville**

Go into an audition thinking, 'You lucky people. I'm really good at this, and I love doing it. I'm well cast, and I'm going to reveal something that you didn't know about the show.' That should send you in the right mood. **Samuel West**

Imagine that you've already got the job: that they've said to you, 'Great, you've got the part – can you just come in and read with the director?'

It takes the pressure off.

Luke Treadaway

Don't think about getting the job: think about the audition as an opportunity to perform in front of an audience. Learn your stuff. Think of two or three different ways of doing it. Be open to suggestions. And above all, don't give yourself a hard time. If you think about getting the job, you'll just open yourself up to huge disappointment when you don't get it. **David Harewood**

At auditions, they will tend to say, 'What do you think of the character?' Make sure you can answer this question politely, even if your character is so bland you feel like saying, 'What? She's just a wife: a stereotype.' **Imogen Stubbs**

Being keen and agreeable gets you a long way. I've often heard directors say that what they want when they're auditioning is someone who's really keen to play the part, and who they think they can work with. Talent isn't necessarily the first thing. **Oliver Ford Davies**

Ninety per cent of an audition can be down to the chat. This person might be doing six weeks of night shoots with you in Leeds: they need to know more about you than just whether you can do the job. Directors generally want to work with actors who are hard-working, prepared, open, friendly and confident. All the actors I've met who keep working have a very open personality that is conducive to standing around with lots of people, playing make-believe. **Luke Treadaway**

Remember that the person auditioning you wants you to be great. When I audition actors for a show I'm directing, I want you to solve my problem. We're not there to make you feel small, insignificant, untalented, frightened. It's up to us to make sure you have a nice time – and if anybody gives you a bad time in audition, avoid them. They might be brisk, and that's fine: they're busy people. But if they're there to humiliate you, take no part in it. **Samuel West**

If you go into an audition wanting a job, it's odds on you won't get it. You're putting out need and desperation, as opposed to a desire to interpret the part your way. Auditions are horrible things: it's awful to stand there being judged. So try psyching yourself up before you go in, thinking that it's about the character on the page, and nothing to do with you. That normally keeps you in a safe place. **Mark Umbers**

Don't be over-emotional. I used to think that if I cried in auditions, it would show them what a good actress I was. Now I just think it's slightly embarrassing. Be as still and simple as possible – and take direction, even if you think what they're saying is bollocks. They will assume most people going in to the audition can act. What they really want to know is if you can take direction. **Imogen Stubbs**

When people ask what you've been up to, tell them – but make it pithy. It's good to say, 'I've just been working at the National and had a good time.' But if people eulogise about the job they've just had, the auditioner ends up thinking, 'Well, you're not going to get this one. Enough of that, please.' **Mark Gatiss**

Have your audition speech prepared rather than your chat. I've been on the other side of things, auditioning actors, and it's a massive turn-off if someone comes in obviously trying to impress. I've seen it all – from actors saying they're really hungover (you will not get the job); to others coming in looking like a bag lady. If you're going to be memorable, it will be because you did a good audition – not because you were the person who came in with loads of coats and bags. **Zawe Ashton**

Don't go on about your own opinions. As a young actor, I was always doing that. For my first audition for the RSC, which I didn't get, I remember walking out and saying to the assistant director, 'How did that go?' And he said, 'Just don't talk too much.' **Simon Russell Beale**

Know when to leave. It's much better to do the audition, be polite, and then get out. I hate all the chit-chat: it's just a waste of everybody's life. They end up getting to know you as you, which makes trying to be somebody different even harder. **Imogen Stubbs**

Don't be afraid to have a conversation. A lot of people think it's just about you getting the job – but you have to work out what *you* think about those people as well. Having a conversation with them about the project is a good way of finding out whether you think they're going to be a good director or a bad director. **Lesley Manville**

One of the things that is very noticeable from my involvement with Equity is that the balance has shifted so much in the last thirty years from workers to bosses. Well, auditions should reverse that trend. It shouldn't feel like the panel is saying, 'You're coming into an oversubscribed profession where absolutely everybody is desperate to do everything for the minimum. We don't have to treat you well, we can keep you waiting, we don't have to keep you warm.' The actor may have a horrible time in the audition, and then not want to do the part: or they may have to do the part, and still have a horrible time. **Samuel West**

A real interest in the project you're auditioning for is a good thing. At one of the first auditions I ever did, with Bill Gaskill, I said, 'This part, Mr Gaskill – this is *me*.' And he gave it to me. It was a real risk – I'd never done anything substantial, and looking back, I think, 'God, how on earth did I have the balls to say that?' But he obviously thought, if this young man wants it so much, perhaps he should have it. **Simon Russell Beale**

Fake indifference. I've been on the other side of the audition table a lot, and you can see when people haven't had an audition for ages: it comes off them in waves. Know your speech well, but don't know it so well that you look desperate. And don't spend time shaking hands with everyone in the room, and then shaking hands with everyone when you leave. That also looks a bit desperate. **Mark Gatiss**

If you'll be singing in the audition, prepare a piece that really suits your voice. You may be given the music in advance, and find – especially if it's a new show – that it's just too high for you, and you're screeching. If so, change the key so that you're singing comfortably; they can always change it permanently if you get the job. There's something very powerful about someone going into an audition situation with an understanding of themselves, and what they can bring to the part. **Jenna Russell**

Choose songs that are appropriate to the show you're auditioning for. If you're going up for *Wicked*, singing Valjean's soliloquy from *Les Misérables* at the age of twenty-three, as I did, is a really stupid idea. **David Thaxton**

5. Getting It Right in Screen Tests

So much of doing well in the acting trade is to do with your audition technique – and it's something a lot of us struggle with. It's not a very natural environment, especially for film and TV: you're there with a camcorder perched on a tripod and three people sat on chairs watching you pretending to stand in a river with a crossbow. It's a constant source of amusement, really. Just try to get an essence of the character, and remember that it's not a memory test. **Luke Treadaway**

Screen tests are a little fight I have with my agent. I always say, 'It's going to give them no indication of what kind of actor I am – particularly someone like myself who is a character actor, and changes quite radically part to part.' I feel I've got nothing to present as myself; very self-conscious and inadequate. I just feel like saying to them, 'Why don't you look at my Macbeth clip on YouTube?' Somehow they usually don't want to. **Antony Sher**

Try to relax and be natural.
Give hints – and I mean hints – of as
many changes of thought and emotion
and personality as possible.

> They may not quite know what
> they are looking for yet, and you
> can give them ideas.

Read books, watch movies
close to the subject:

> anything that leads you to believe
> of your character, **'This could
> be me.'**

> In the end, you and the character
> have to merge. Just playing
> everything as you is wrong –

and imitating a character with none of
you at the heart is wrong also.

Harriet Walter

6. Keeping Things in Perspective

Tell yourself the panel love you, even if they look hostile. Tell yourself you have something unique and interesting to offer them. Don't imitate anyone else. You are a new and novel ingredient they didn't even know they were lacking till they saw you... Well, acting is all about make-believe, so make them believe it. **Harriet Walter**

Auditioning is an ongoing learning process: it's not like, 'Ah, I've cracked auditions now, off I go.' You do get actors who admit that they're really good at auditions – it's a gift they have. But most of us just have to keep on working at it. **David Thaxton**

I hated auditions. I was never very good at just getting up and doing a speech into mid-air, or to a chair. I always wished that I could be given parts because people had seen me play other parts. That is, in fact, how I have got most of the parts I've played. **Antony Sher**

After thirty-five years, I've concluded that ultimately, the only thing you can ever be in an audition is you. Bring yourself and your feelings towards whatever you're auditioning for. Sometimes that's going to match with the director's vision, and sometimes it's not – but at least you're giving a genuine version of yourself. You may not be right for that role, but you could very much be right for something that comes up in six months' time. **Jenna Russell**

I'm hopeless at auditions. I can count on two hands the number of parts I've got that way.

On an audition, I wouldn't get into an amateur production of *Bunty Pulls the Strings*.

Bill Paterson

If you want to create work for yourself, you've got to realise that when you go to an audition, you have to be centred in what you do, and not worry too much about the end result. Of course we want to impress – but you need to breathe deeply, and develop your inner core. **Brian Cox**

Be yourself, as much as you can. That, in the end, is what people are looking for. There's such a limited amount you can tell from an audition: whether people have vocal impediments; whether they seem uncomfortable. But most of all, directors and casting agents are on the lookout for someone who has interesting qualities, interesting instincts: interesting, I mean, because they are true to themselves. **Simon Callow**

Typecasting – and How to Live with It

We all make snap judgements about people. For actors, this can prove frustrating – especially when they're being asked to play the same part time after time just because they happen to look, in casting directors' minds, like a doctor, or an estate agent, or a psychopath. Here are a few words from the Players on how to avoid typecasting – or even turn it to your advantage.

Accept that you're always going to be on a list with people of a similar ilk. It starts when you start: you immediately go onto a list with people of around your age, your height, your colouring, your background. As you go up for work, you'll find they'll also be there – there was a time when I could always expect a couple of my siblings to be at auditions [McGann is one of four brothers, all of whom are actors]. But the good thing about this is that if you're on a list of five or six people, it stands to reason that you're going to get a turn eventually. He might get the gig this time – but next time, it could be you.
Paul McGann

There's a continuum between soap-opera actors, who play a version of themselves; and people like Simon Russell Beale, who can genuinely play a whole array of different characters. Accept which kind of actor you are – and don't worry if it's more the soap-opera type. Soaps need actors who are able to be as natural as possible. **Jo Brand**

Try to escape your pigeonhole. A lot of stereotyping goes on with casting, especially in TV and film. Casting directors worry about whether an actor looks like a plumber, a vicar, or a governor of the Bank of England: will the audience accept in the first ten seconds that this person is who he says he is? That's difficult for an actor to cope with: you may be grateful that they've thought of you again as a vicar or a mad scientist, but sometimes, you may just need to say no to yet another of those parts, and do something else. A good agent will help you to do this. **Oliver Ford Davies**

Don't allow yourself to be put in a box. For a while after I left college, I was just 'young posh bloke'. That's a very difficult thing to shake off, especially when I'm not like that in real life. But oddly, ever since I've predominantly played Americans. I think that's good: every time I read something very English, it feels like I could play that part standing on my head. **Mark Umbers**

You're in trouble if you go against what casting directors think you can do. You might be in denial about something.

Luckily or unluckily, I've always known what my **strengths** are, and worked on my **weaknesses**: I'm not a beautiful soprano singer, for instance. The people who are casting you aren't stupid. They tend to be right.

Tracie Bennett

As a young actor, you've got to go with what you're given. Casting directors aren't very imaginative, and we tend to get hired because of the thing we did before: when I was younger, I played a couple of soldier boys, and for two years, that was all I got offered. It would be lovely to start with a manifesto, as a twenty-year-old, and say, 'I'm only going to play these parts.' But of course you won't work. So just go with it, and find out what your appeal is.
Paul McGann

Learning to Say No

'No' isn't a word that comes readily to most actors, especially those just starting out. It's important to remain as open as possible to your director's vision, and to the great variety of work that may come your way – but where should you draw the line between keeping an open mind, and being asked to do something that makes you uncomfortable? What if your agent is putting you up for parts you just don't want? And is it ever worth taking work that's unpaid or profit-share? Our Players share their advice on how, and when, to say no.

Accept virtually anything – even if it isn't the kind of thing you want to do. When you're starting out, virtually all experience is useful. Don't wait for the perfect thing. If it's porn films or something, you've probably got to think twice. But don't be snooty – you just daren't, in this profession. **Jane Asher**

Be very cautious about working for free. Acting is an art, and it requires health in body and in mind: and there are serious consequences to the demographic of the profession if companies require people to work for free. But if you really want to take an unpaid part, talk to the producers, and find out whether they're making money and their actors aren't. If it's a profit-share, fine – but make sure it's a fair one. And meanwhile, join the union! **Samuel West**

If you're working in musical theatre, be very careful of working for just one producer. You can end up skipping from show to show to show. Be wary of that: it's important to spread your employers. **Jenna Russell**

Be open-minded about what you can do. It's easy to say 'only do things that you're passionate about', but obviously financial needs create other needs. I've done plenty of rubbish TV because I've had to earn money. But if there ever comes a time when you can just about get by, it's good to only do roles that will really challenge you. My only criterion now is: will it make me better as an actor? That can be to do with the part, or who you're working opposite. Forget about the money and everything else, if you can. **Mark Umbers**

Remember that making a living is what creates the distinction between amateur and professional. I can call myself a professional actor because I don't do anything else. **Samuel West**

Only understudy a couple of times at most. Then take a deep breath and say, 'I'm not going to do it any more.' If you're a very good understudy, they will want to keep you. So there always comes a point where, if you aspire to be the lead, you have to take a deep breath and say no. **Jenna Russell**

I don't believe in making actors work for nothing.

I know people who have done it and have got professional work out of it. But I'd say to them,

> 'You're not a professional actor while you're working for free.'

Julie Walters

Don't be afraid of saying no. I've never done a sex scene, thank God – although I did once get sent a really filthy script. I was the head of an old people's home, having an affair with a gardener; there was a scene featuring me sat on top of him, naked, in wild abandon. I just said to my agent, 'I think not.' We all know our limits. If thinking about doing something brings up goosebumps, don't do it. **Jo Brand**

Know when to use your power of veto. If your instinct says, 'Actually, good as this looks, I'd rather be elsewhere', go with it. There's very little in this job that actually feels creative: you're not writing the stuff, or producing it: it's just coming down the line at you. So turn the stuff down that might get you stuck in a cul de sac. I did that at twenty-three, with the first TV series I was involved with for the BBC. They wanted me to do a second series, and I said no. Everybody thought I was mad. But within a few months, I got the thing I really wanted. **Paul McGann**

Don't turn a part down because you're scared of not being good. You might be missing the chance to explore something different. Once, a play was sent to me by Simon Stephens, in which it said, 'the main character is a thirty-year-old Manchester taxi driver'. I thought, 'That's just ludicrous' – and then I decided just to work very hard at my Manchester accent and do it. If somebody wants you to do something, it's because they think you can do it. It's not for you to judge. **Simon Russell Beale**

We forget, as actors, that we have a choice. It's difficult to see that sometimes, because we don't like to say no. But you *can* say no. And sometimes saying no is a really good, positive thing. Listen to your gut. If your gut tells you not to do it, don't do it. Something else will come along. **Jenna Russell**

I've never done a sex scene, but I've had to roll around on a bed with my top off a couple of times. You can say no, but it might cost you the job. When I was in *The Turn of the Screw* for the BBC, they said, 'We need to see his bottom.' I got into a complete state about it – but luckily, they ended up not doing it anyway. **Mark Umbers**

Coping with Rejection

There isn't an actor in the world who hasn't gone up for a part they longed to play, and then seen it go to someone else. The rejection can often feel intensely personal: it's as if the casting director or director has spent time with you, assessing your appearance, your voice, your delivery, and then found you wanting. Learning to bounce back from these inevitable disappointments is a hard lesson – and one all our Players have studied for many years. Here, they discuss the best ways to dust yourself off and keep on going.

Remember that you will fail in ninety-nine out of a hundred auditions. All actors do. **Jane Asher**

Get tough. When you're rejected as an actor, it's in a very personal way. I also write books and paint paintings, and having a book or a painting disliked is slightly different from having yourself – the way you sound, the way you look – rejected. So you've just got to toughen up. **Antony Sher**

Cling on to the fact that auditions are not a test of your talent. If you're one of the people that the casting director has put in front of the director – and for film and television, he or she may only be seeing four or five people for each part – the director is assuming that you are a good actor. Increasingly, then, the audition is really about whether you correspond to the idea that the director already has about the part. You will walk in the room, and the director may think, 'Too tall, too short, too fat, too thin, too brunette, too blond…' He or she will go through their paces, but you know the decision has already been made. So the best way to cope with rejection is to keep saying to yourself, 'This isn't about my ability, my talent; it's about whether in some way my pheromones are right for the way the director sees the part.' **Oliver Ford Davies**

There's a philosophical nature to acting. My mother used to say, 'What's for you will not go by you.' It's a great phrase to keep in mind when you don't get a job. **Brian Cox**

Get used to rejection. You'll constantly be knocked back – on a weekly or daily basis. If you can't handle that, it will just torment you. People call acting a competitive profession, but really it's more accurate to say it's indifferent. It doesn't care for your youthful sense of uniqueness. You might be trying this because you were the best at your school. And sure enough, you might have been – but once you're out there, you're going to meet every other kid who was the best at their school. **Paul McGann**

So much is luck; so much is random. You take one job, and two weeks later you're approached about something that would have been the perfect job for you. You just need to make peace with that, I'm afraid. **Imogen Stubbs**

Even if you don't get the job, you have contributed to the life of the show by auditioning. You may have just been so terrible that the director came out and thought, 'Well, whatever it is, it's not *that.*' Or maybe you've taught the director something he or she didn't know about the play. Either way, you have contributed to the life – the art – of this show. Always console yourself with this when you don't get a job. Because even if you're great at auditions, you're probably only going to get one in five, or even one in thirty. **Samuel West**

Accept that you may need time to grow into yourself. My first director, Peter Dews – a very experienced TV and film director, who ran the Birmingham Rep – said to me when I was twenty-seven, 'You'll be all right when you're forty, and even better when you're fifty.' He was absolutely right. At the age of fifty, I was doing *Racing Demon* at the National Theatre. **Oliver Ford Davies**

Trust that things will come at the right time. Sometimes it's better not to get that big lead at the RSC when you're just starting out: you might be better at it four years on. **Jenna Russell**

Don't think that all other actors are getting work – it will be painful when you see other people getting agents, and parts. But if you're absolutely determined, just keep trying. There isn't enough work for everybody – but there are also not that many actors out there who are truly wonderful. If you are any good, hopefully you will be picked up eventually. **Jane Asher**

It's often said that companies like the RSC and the National don't promote from within – the problem can be that you go in playing a small part, and then they don't employ you again. That can be hard. I remember, for example, that in my first year at the RSC, Ken Stott was in the company, playing small parts, and complaining most of the time. Ken left as soon as he could, and I thought, 'You've no idea what an unusual and remarkable actor Ken Stott is.' So don't think these companies are the be-all and end-all. **Oliver Ford Davies**

Remember that it can all change so quickly. You can be having the best time, then hit a blank where nobody wants to audition you, and you think it's all over. But it does change. **Jenna Russell**

It's really hard to come second. I know the feeling. There's no good way round it other than to do another job. **Samuel West**

PREPARING
THE PART

Building a Character

Every actor has his or her own means of getting under a character's skin – it might be Method-style immersion, watching relevant films or TV shows, or poring over books that describe the script's location or period setting. Here are some dos and don'ts on bringing your character to life.

Research doesn't necessarily make you a better actor. You can play a part in Chekhov without knowing anything about Russia. You might not do it very well, but you can certainly do it. **Imogen Stubbs**

There are no rules for how you research a character. Some actors research intensively and come out with the most brilliant performances – but I don't tend to research a lot intellectually. I always assume that what you need is in the play – or should be – unless you need to perfect a specific skill. If you've got to look as if you've been a steel welder all your life, you may need to go and watch a steel welder to get it right. **Jane Asher**

Children are the best actors.
     A child doesn't pretend to
     be a train: a child is a train;
he or she has absolutely no
inhibitions about it.

Keep hold of that child
within you throughout
your whole life as an
actor.

Children don't research roles.
     They don't stand around a
     film set practising accents
     for days on end.

They either do it or they don't.
     And if they do it, it is in
     their own individual way.

Brian Cox

Respond to each project in the way that the project requires. You have to be adaptable enough to know that if somebody wants to do a small-scale Shakespeare, that's different from doing a large-scale Shakespeare. And if somebody's doing Chekhov, it's different from doing Shakespeare full stop. **Simon Russell Beale**

If you like research, do it. If you're playing a rocket scientist, find out what a rocket scientist does; if you're playing a traffic warden, ask them, 'What's it like to have people spit at you?' Read a book, go and see a few movies, read a similar play. But be sparing. When you go into rehearsals, the director wants you to trace an emotional journey, not bump into the furniture and remember your lines. He or she doesn't need to hear your research. **Lenny Henry**

Break routines. Take a different route home. Put yourself in unfamiliar situations. Let in the lateral thinking. Watch someone who is nearer your character than you are: maybe even follow and befriend them (don't stalk them!). **Harriet Walter**

Before you even think about a script or a play, you need to think about people. Actors should be experts in character. That is our job, really, more than anything else, so we should be observing all the time. Trying to figure out what it feels like to be this person or that person; what sort of physical or emotional or intellectual experience they have. Then try it all on for size. **Simon Callow**

Acting isn't showing, it's doing. To build a character, you need to change the way you do things, or the intention with which you do them. Observe the people around you: ask yourself why they are here, what they're talking about, how long they've been together. Then think about what your character does, and, most importantly *how* he or she does it. **Samuel West**

Some parts simply need to be played from the heart. That's how it was for me with Arnold, the New York drag queen who is the main character in Harvey Fierstein's great *Torch Song Trilogy*. He's a very exotic character, and very far from my own experience, but I did hardly any research for him at all. My main job was simply to work with what was written, using whatever I could bring to him from my own heart. **Antony Sher**

Approach the part in the same way you approach the production. How is the director choosing to direct this particular show? What will be useful? There are certain things you should always know: your time-line; your parentage; your background. Add in anything else that, frankly, makes you feel less of a fraud. **Samuel West**

Try wearing your character's shoes. I always find my way into a character physically: if I'm doing a stage play, I speak to wardrobe very early on and say, 'I need to be wearing the shoes that the character's wearing.' And with my character Estes in [the US TV series] *Homeland*, I couldn't rehearse without being in a suit: it just seemed wrong. **David Harewood**

Many actors will tell you different things about characters. Famously, Beryl Reid always started with the shoes. Other people start with the accent, or the position of the spine; or they try to link the character to a particular animal. But the truth is that all these things really do one thing – make you move and feel differently to who you are yourself. You'll never cease to be yourself, of course – your body is your body: I could never be tall; I could never, alas, be slim – but you can be many different things to the way you are when you're walking down the street. **Simon Callow**

Take your character and fill her with the things you know intimately: the things that connect the two of you. Say to yourself, 'If I'd taken that same avenue, this could have been my life.' I remember doing a part at the Donmar years ago, and finding that the character was just like my grandmother. Watching films and reading books can be helpful – but in the end, it's got to come from you. **Helen Baxendale**

Look at the script very carefully. Ask yourself what this person is saying, and why he or she is saying it in this particular way. What is it about them that makes them speak the way they do? The more questions you ask, the more you get the flavour of what it is that they're saying. You need to develop a sensitivity in yourself to the idea of character, so that you can start to feel the way they feel, move the way they move, and then speak the way they speak. **Simon Callow**

Make a playlist on your computer of the sort of music that you think your character would listen to, and then listen to it all the time. My playlist for Othello was quite dark – Mahler, Screaming Jay Hawkins: things that would get me into a dark mood. If you're paying a flibbertigibbet clown, play very light, flibbertigibbet music. It's up to you. **Lenny Henry**

Be prepared to research specific aspects of your character. When I played Leontes, for instance, I thought about the irrational jealousy he has about his wife having an affair. He is sometimes dismissed as a stage villain, but I set myself a research course – interviewing psychiatrists and all sorts of people – and discovered that there is a particular mental condition called morbid or sexual jealousy that reflects, symptom by symptom, what Shakespeare wrote for Leontes. Something like that can completely transform the way you play a character. **Antony Sher**

Some parts simply do not need research. If you get a brilliant speech, you think, 'I know this person: I don't need to research it.' It just comes off the page and into your heart. But sometimes you do need to research some specific background. When I played Mo Mowlam, for instance, I couldn't remember how she spoke, so I looked at a lot of footage of her; I found out a little bit about her illness. But I didn't need to go and live in the Houses of Parliament and become an MP to make that script work. **Julie Walters**

Peter Brook once said, 'Don't think you can play yourself.' Sometimes you look at a part and think, 'Well, this is me, so I don't need to do much.' But as Brook warns, very often, nothing happens. All acting is a rearrangement of yourself. You can't literally become another person, but you can access your own feelings and thoughts, and rearrange them to accommodate this other person. In that sense, all acting is character acting. **Oliver Ford Davies**

There are no 'shoulds' when it comes to researching a character. If you're dealing with a very specific world or period of history that's unknown or alien to you, then research is very important. But if the play is very much a playwright's creative invention, however based in history, then research into the actual historical character is only really useful to your curiosity. You have to play the character as conceived by the writer – with, of course, your own imagination giving it individuality and personal truth. **Harriet Walter**

The voice is crucial. I'm nowhere until I can get the voice of a character. That's how I write, as well. If I can hear a character, I can write them. It's really the same principle with acting. **Mark Gatiss**

Find the character's speaking voice first. To find Adelaide's voice for *Guys and Dolls*, first I went back to her era, and then I thought about the fact she had a cold, and settled on this husky, high speaking voice. Then I had to sing from that voice. I don't like seeing a musical where the actors speak in a certain voice, and then the singing voice sounds completely different. **Tracie Bennett**

Character is really about the way you do things. I always start by making four lists: what other people say about you, what the author says about you, what you say about yourself, and what you say about other people. With a big part, it can be quite boring: but if you don't do it, you'll be in the third week of rehearsal and go, 'Oh, she's my cousin! Oh, *now* I see!' **Samuel West**

Keep reading the play. Slowly, by osmosis, you will be making decisions, without having to force them. It's about relaxation: allowing decisions to be made without imposing them. Imagine and research the period and the character's background. Create a backstory. Ask yourselves questions. And once you've got all those things in place, relax and let things happen. **Samantha Spiro**

Find pictures that are apposite to the play, and stick them up in your dressing room. When I was doing Othello, I had pictures of James Earl Jones playing Othello stuck up everywhere, and lots of quotes from the text. Pick anything you think will inspire you. **Lenny Henry**

Read as much about the show and your character as you can. If it's based on real life, you need to know everything it's possible to know about that person. If it's based on source material, read it. The number of people who were in *Les Mis* when I was, and hadn't read the book, was insane. I remember being in rehearsals once and someone said, 'My name's Pierre.' I was like, 'No it's not – you're Jean Prouvaire. You're in the programme: there's a whole page dedicated to your character.' This actor was blissfully unaware of what he was doing, and who he was. **David Thaxton**

You can do as much research as you like, but ultimately it's a question of piss or get off the pot. You see actors who research roles and get wonderful detail. But it should be there in the work. We underestimate the power of imagination; the power of make-believe. **Brian Cox**

If a character really flies off the page, you can just act on instinct. Sometimes all the flesh is already in the script, and it's your job just to nail it. **Mark Umbers**

First, mine the factual information out of the script, and then start to add the layers: what's called the 'magic if'. Keep your antennae up for things that resonate. I'm extremely affected by images: when I did Ionesco's *Rhinoceros* at the Royal Court, I looked at lots of photographs and listened to a lot of music. It's good if the music has a double edge to it: it helps get into the character's complexity. *Rhinoceros* is set in the 1950s, but I found myself listening to a lot of grime. **Zawe Ashton**

Keep what's the same and change what's different. People often say you should lose yourself in the character, but it's actually about doing the opposite – *finding* yourself in the character. You need to know yourself well enough to say, 'Yes, he or she is very like me in this respect; on the other hand, we're quite different.' **Samuel West**

Read books, watch movies close to the subject: anything that leads you to believe of your character, 'This could be me.' In the end, you and the character have to merge. Just playing everything as you is wrong – and imitating a character with none of you at the heart is wrong also. **Harriet Walter**

Playing difficult characters is a privilege. I once had a crisis where I was sick of playing nasty people. Then I realised there was another way of looking at it. It's a privilege because you begin to understand who these people are: where that hatred comes from. And that in itself is a very useful thing. **Brian Cox**

Go through the script and write down all the facts about your character – everything that is definitely true. Then write down all the questions you have. By finding the answer to each question, you're unlocking all these different things about him. You start to get a feeling for what it is that's the engine of that character – for what's really driving him. **Luke Treadaway**

Play the opposite. The performances I'm always drawn to, and the delivery that feels most truthful to me, are when the line says one thing, and the actor is thinking another. I'm a great believer, too, in people not being one single thing: it's their complexity that I most enjoy working out. With Vod, my character in Channel 4's *Fresh Meat*, for instance, I saw her strength on the page, so the first thing I worked out was, 'Where's her vulnerability?' It makes for much better characters. **Zawe Ashton**

It's fun to have a working knowledge of the past. It's a privilege that is given to few people in this life. If you know what year your character was born, why not find out what was on the radio? It might be fun. Do whatever you think is exciting, and doesn't feel like boring homework. **Samuel West**

Make choices about who your character is, what he wants, and where he's going. Make big, bold, brave choices: they're the interesting ones. **David Thaxton**

All we're trying to do, as actors, is be believable and interesting to watch. There are so many ways to get to that. Some people are very instinctive, and don't read books or go to museums. I'm not in that category. To play Christopher in *The Curious Incident of the Dog in the Night-Time*, for example, I went to five different schools for kids with autism; I watched hundreds of documentaries and read loads of books. When I was doing the play, it wasn't that

I was thinking about the time I spent at those schools, but it made me feel more confident and prepared. **Luke Treadaway**

Look for every character's secret. No one might ever work it out from your performance, but it will root your feet on the stage. **Zawe Ashton**

Actors are like transmitting machines. Stuff should come through you in such a way that you don't identify with it. If you do identify with it, you're not doing the job properly. I watch well-known actors get up and do TV programmes about characters they play. They've invented this whole ridiculous life for them. I feel like saying, 'Hang on, it's only a role. Get a sense of perspective. What you do is great, but you give the profession a bad rap.' It's a great profession in many ways, you see, but it's not rocket science. **Brian Cox**

Lines –
and When to Learn Them

Is it best to turn up on the first day of rehearsals word-perfect – or do most directors prefer you to learn your lines gradually? Should you draft in a friend to run your lines with you, or just practise saying them in the bathroom mirror? Here, the Players offer their tips on how, when and where to commit that script to memory.

Don't use the rehearsal time to learn your lines. Some actors spend their time stumbling over lines. You learn your lines at home: otherwise everybody's waiting for you to mess about with your memory. **Julie Walters**

Know your lines backwards, especially when you're working on a film. You might think you know the script, but once you're in that studio, under the lights, with a whole team of people being paid by the hour, it all gets very tense, and the words tend to disappear. You've got to turn up knowing it inside out. **Jane Asher**

Learn your lines with a friend the night before filming. Say them looking into your friend's eyes. Your friend will be distracting you.

You will think you know the scene because you can do it looking at the floor, but human contact is distracting – and you want there to be human contact when you film the scene.

Samuel West

Make your partner run your lines with you, if you have one. Learning your lines is more difficult if you're single. Drag a neighbour in to help, or a friend. Or try recording yourself saying all the other characters' lines, leaving gaps between them for you to say your own. **Tracie Bennett**

People will say there's a disadvantage to learning your lines before day one of rehearsals. There isn't: they're just being lazy. Knowing your lines sends a message to the company. It allows you to put your book down. There are some actors who won't learn their lines so that a director can't give them notes. Those are the actors who won't get employed again. **Samuel West**

Talk to the director before starting rehearsals, and find out whether he or she wants you to learn the script in advance. Some directors will definitely want you to – Michael Grandage is one of them. His reasoning, and it's one I agree with, is that it's a real bonus to be able to put the script down as soon as you can. But some scripts are just really tricky to learn. I found Arnold Wesker's *Chicken Soup with Barley* particularly difficult, for some reason: I was holding the script until quite far into rehearsals. **Samantha Spiro**

Learn your lines when the director tells you to. The director will sometimes say, 'I want everybody to be off the book by the first day of rehearsals': so do

that. Try writing your lines out, at least ten times for each scene. Or repeat them, or have somebody run them with you. However you do it, you need to be off the book when the director says you should be.
Lenny Henry

The Dos and Don'ts
of Rehearsal

The rehearsal room: that empty space in which you, and the rest of your ensemble, will build the play together. Well, that might be how it feels if rehearsals are going well. But how do you cope if the rehearsal period proves tricky? Should you openly contradict the director? And is it ever okay to make suggestions about your fellow actor's performance? The Players share the wisdom they've acquired in countless rehearsal rooms.

Love the rehearsal period. Be prepared to make a fool of yourself; listen to the director and the writing. Sometimes it comes together so easily, and sometimes it's like you're not all in the same play. Go in and give the director some choices – then he can play with you. **Tracie Bennett**

Listen and absorb as much as possible. You learn so much from watching: it's fascinating how differently actors work. **Jane Asher**

Rehearsal is a harrowing process.

> You lose your bearings: you can't fail to, especially if you're working on a new play, or work which is new to you.

But it's also an extraordinary time of sowing seeds which will develop later.

Simon Callow

You will learn what *not* to do by watching others, as well as what to do. You can be watching somebody do something, and know what they're doing wrong. A siren will go off in your brain. **Mark Umbers**

Don't be scared to ask for help. **Lenny Henry**

Be a social animal. I certainly work best in sociable atmospheres. You get that much more with theatre than with film – it's great to be in a room for six weeks rehearsing with a whole bunch of actors, rather than sitting there on set in your little hutch. **Paul McGann**

If you have a main role, you need to lead from the front and make bold choices. I once did a play called *Orpheus Descending*: I had to decide whether to do my part in a Deep South accent, or an Italian one. At the readthrough, I went for Italian. I can remember everyone looking at me; I probably sounded like the Wall's Cornetto advertisement. But it went very well in the end. You've just got to plunge in. **Imogen Stubbs**

Keep open. Don't be too rigid. Everything will change not only from part to part, but also with each group of people you work with. You must constantly be open to the other actors, the director, and the writer. **Antony Sher**

Leave your phone outside the rehearsal room. A rehearsal room is a little like a therapy session: things will be discussed that should remain in the room. It's rather worrying if your fellow actors are all sitting there playing with their phones. **Bill Paterson**

Don't do your research during rehearsal time. I don't like people who come in and mess about for eight hours, or sit there reading a book. Research is your homework. During rehearsals, you should be talking about the text: that's what you're there to do. **Tracie Bennett**

I love watching other people work. There's something intriguing about somebody doing a light sketch of the character, and each time they come back to the scene, it's getting more and more defined. It's a great privilege, being in a rehearsal room. It's magic. **Jenna Russell**

The actor is both laboratory scientist and laboratory rat. We test ourselves under different conditions. We undergo the experiment *and* we observe and recreate the results. **Harriet Walter**

Don't throw the baby out with the bath water. Usually, when you first read the play, your instincts about it will be very good: you've probably understood it right away, and then you might spend five weeks messing it up. It's like life-drawing, which I do occasionally. If I just do a quick sketch, it's usually okay.

But if I work at it for three hours, I may start to destroy what I've done. **Imogen Stubbs**

Be sponge-like. Keep yourself open to being affected by the other actors and the director: they may be wanting to push you into a completely different direction to the one you had in mind. **Samantha Spiro**

There's always that stage during rehearsals when you think, 'I can't do this.' Then, at a certain point, you come through that into the sunshine. The great thing is that you never know when that will be. **Tracie Bennett**

Watch the people you're on stage with. Oddly, I think I've learnt most from women, perhaps because I'm not in any way in competition with them. I've learnt a lot from Judi Dench, from Juliet Stevenson. So when you get into a rehearsal room with an experienced, good actor, just watch how they rehearse and build up a part. **Oliver Ford Davies**

Don't lose your instincts. Really, they're the only thing you've got. Sometimes you will need to fight your corner and go, 'I think you're wrong about that.' It's always worth making sure both that you have a good angle on something, and that you're flexible. It's a balance, always. **Julie Walters**

Allow your imagination to wander freely while rehearsing. Sitting on the bus, waiting for a Tube, going off to sleep at night: the subconscious mind is clever at picking up ideas and inspiration, and filtering out what is not useful. If a dream or imagined scene about a character has come from your own mind, it links you deeply to that character. **Harriet Walter**

I'm a stickler for correct English. I'm over-fussy. If a script isn't saying quite what I want it to say, I will interfere. It's great if you get a wonderful writer like Alan Ayckbourn, who, like me, is a stickler for every word. I did once get him to change one word before he published the script. I was so thrilled. **Jane Asher**

Giving another actor notes is unforgivable. There was once an actor, who shall remain nameless, with whom I had fantastic chemistry on stage; but in between scenes, he would be giving me notes. It was just gobsmacking. Once another actor has said something to you, you're undermined. It's a really bad thing to do, but it's something older actors quite often do to younger actors. **Imogen Stubbs**

I'm always happy to get notes from anybody – even other members of the cast. They might see something you don't: you can't always stand outside yourself and see what you're doing. **Jane Asher**

Learn from each other. When I'm rehearsing, I don't expect young actors to sit in awe of the older actor who's been doing it for ever: I get as much out of working with them as, hopefully, they get out of working with me. A good rehearsal process creates an atmosphere where you're all speaking the same language, and bringing your combined talents to make this event work. **Lesley Manville**

Rehearsal is not a place for getting things right, it's a place for getting things wrong. With that in mind, you should try almost everything that is suggested to you. **Samuel West**

Really trust your fellow actors, and have them trust you. If something goes wrong, they will help you and get you out of trouble. That's what rehearsals are for: you learn to trust the other person to be there when they should be, and to give you the right cue. **Lenny Henry**

Have a sense of your own self-worth – but don't arrive with your character, and your decisions about them, fully formed, because then you've got nowhere to go. **Mark Gatiss**

GETTING
IT RIGHT

Making Use
of Technique

Stanislavsky, Lee Strasberg, David Mamet: the theoreti-
cians of acting are numerous, and every drama school or
training course has its favourites. But how do you decide
which techniques work best for you, and then draw on them
to deliver a great performance? Do the best actors succeed
by hard graft or flashes of inspiration? And how can you
improve your vocal technique, and ensure your lines reach
the back of the Olivier stalls? Here's where our Players get
technical…

I am into Method acting, but only when it's necessary. It's like Olivier famously saying, 'Why don't you
try acting?' There's great truth in that. **Julie Walters**

Learn to cry to order. Richard E. Grant is great at
that. I timed him once – it took seven seconds for
tears to come out of his eyes. I, on the other hand,
need a crying stick. It contains very strong menthol:
you put it under your eye, close to the eyeball, and
it makes tears come out. A lot of people use those.
Jo Brand

Technique is very useful, but I don't believe you can teach somebody the brilliance that an actor like Simon Russell Beale has.

With the really great actors, it's just there.

It's about truth – or the appearance of truth.

Real truth, of course, is very dangerous: Daniel Day Lewis, famously, saw his dead father while playing Hamlet.

That's where technique comes in. You have to have technique, or you would go completely mad.

Jane Asher

At drama school, they showed us a little vocal-technique trick. It's an imaginative one. Visualise the distance between the stage and the back of the theatre – in some theatres, that could be forty or fifty metres. There are people sitting back there who've paid £25 a ticket. If you can imagine that distance, and you want to be heard, you'll be heard all right. But remember that there's a difference between shouting and speaking audibly. You have to fire your imagination – you can cross those distances with your voice only once you understand what the distances are. **Paul McGann**

Acting is about losing your self-consciousness. I've never really been able to do that. I did a television documentary about kissing once. I went to RADA, and acted out a scene with some students, which finished with a kiss between the two actors in each little group. They paired me with a delightful young man of twenty. When it came to the kiss, I just couldn't do it – but the other actors were all writhing around on the floor. Good actors are able to abandon themselves in a way that your average upright person just can't. **Jo Brand**

I do kissing scenes all the time, for some reason. It is sometimes a bit weird the first time you do it. But remember that it's not you, it's the person you're playing. You've got to be disciplined about it. **Mark Umbers**

Acting, like all the creative arts, is about **imagination** and **craft; passion** and **discipline**.

Imagination and passion will only carry you so far, and craft and technique will carry you so far: you've really got to be able to combine the two.

It's a difficult balance – **and it's something that you're constantly striving for**.

Oliver Ford Davies

Have a couple of different accents in your pocket. I now have a couple of American accents, reflecting different places and classes. Practise, practise, practise: watch movies, read a newspaper aloud in your American accent. Watch accent-coach videos on the internet. And try to run it past a native speaker if you can. When I'm in the US, I often go out and pretend to be American. A lot of people in both Britain and America have no idea I'm British, so I guess it's been working. **David Harewood**

Avoid speechifying. John Gielgud discovered, as he got older, that he really didn't like the younger Gielgud: he thought he overdid it. It's true that at the end of his life, Gielgud was the greater verse speaker. Sometimes I see actors nowadays – even some who have done rather well – and think, 'Why are you acting like that: *describing* what you're doing as opposed to *doing* it?' It makes me want to reach for the sick bucket. **Brian Cox**

Most people can access their emotions. They know what anger and love and jealousy and all these things are about. Acting is about deciding how to communicate that. **Oliver Ford Davies**

Find the emotional centre of your character. This is something that John Gillett goes into in his book on Stanislavsky. He talks about giving the emotional centre of the character a location, shape, texture, material, colour and temperature. So if you imagine that your character's emotional centre is a small, two-inch, perfectly spherical steel ball in the front of your forehead, you're going to be a very different person from somebody who has an eighteen-inch fuzzy warm ball of light between their hipbones. **Samuel West**

Try actioning. It comes from the Stanislavsky method, but you can bend it to your own instincts. It involves applying an active verb to each statement in the script. Take the line 'Can I get you a drink?' We all know what the literal meaning is, but you might add the action, 'I seduce you.' It ain't easy – but it's so useful. **Zawe Ashton**

Breathe from wherever feels comfortable for you. I remember being at the RSC and going to a voice coach: I found it so confusing, because they told me that the way I was breathing was completely wrong. I was so stiff and uncomfortable. In the end I thought, 'No, I can walk about and speak and breathe the way I've been breathing for the last twenty-five years.' **Jenna Russell**

Don't neglect your vocal technique. I worked with a wonderful teacher called Kristin Linklater: probably one of the best voice teachers ever. She talked about finding your breathing centre: that it all came from your solar plexus. It's this – your physical inner core – that gives you the support you need. **Brian Cox**

Vocal coaches are very useful. I'm crap at vocal technique: always have been. I just try opening my throat and remembering to breathe. **Julie Walters**

Never try to get a result: do it for the work itself. I know actors who do it for self-aggrandising reasons. But I hardly ever watch any of the films I do, because I like being in the moment, filming the scene. It's like playing house as a child. When you played house with your pals, you didn't stop and turn round and say, 'Well, I think that went jolly well.' Children submerge themselves into the moment. And that's what an actor should do, too. **Brian Cox**

Study all the different techniques, but don't forget to use your instincts. If you think about it too much, it makes you a bit wooden; it's like you're outside it. Take an actor like Mark Rylance. You look at him and you can't see the links. The character comes through first, and the writing is so eloquent in his mouth, whatever style he's doing. Now you tell me: is that instinct or technique, or both? **Tracie Bennett**

I've never got too lost in the theory of acting – Meisner, Stanislavsky. My background is largely in agitprop, Brechtian theatre. It was all the rage in the late sixties and early seventies, and I was part of that. I still think that a cast working together is the most wonderful thing. **Bill Paterson**

To me, a born actor will, when they're talking to somebody, start to shift their own shape, and take the shape of the person they're talking to.

They're just irresistibly tempted to find out what it's like to be somebody else.

Simon Callow

Overacting is the enemy. It's easy to fall into that trap: I've been guilty of it, certainly. The minute you learn that you can just be still, and react to things in a normal way, it's like a whole new world opens up for you. **Lenny Henry**

I don't use any official techniques: nothing like Stanislavsky, or anything like that. I use whatever I need for a particular part. If the part is very emotional, I may need to use emotional recall. Or I might require a particular skill: to play Cyrano de Bergerac, who has to be the best swordsman in France, I had to do months of training. That was a particular challenge: I'm a little wimp who never played sport at school. **Antony Sher**

Be very, very careful if you are a Method actor. I definitely feel something when I'm playing a tragedy – you have to, to produce tears, or any kind of sadness. But I'm also thinking about what I'm going to cook for supper tonight. Unless you are deeply 'Method', you have to be existing on two or three levels at once. You can't live through the trauma of a dead child, or whatever it is, every night. **Jane Asher**

I'll always remember a great teacher who taught a class called 'Stanisvlasky and Onwards'. He was very eccentric. He once cast me by walking in a room with his head down saying, 'I'm looking for a pair of legs: there they are.' They were my legs. **Brian Cox**

Acting for Stage

Most actors value working in the theatre above all else —
even though the dressing rooms are usually poky, the pay
abysmal, and the prospect of hundreds of people hanging
off your every word pretty terrifying. So how should you
try to get the most out of working on stage? How do you
build a good rapport with the audience? And how do you
ensure you're happy and well on stage, night after night?

People often ask which I prefer: film or theatre?
The only real difference is that you can learn things
working in theatre that will stand you in good stead
the next time you're on a film set. It doesn't work
the other way round, though. There's nothing you
can learn on a film set that will help you the next
time you step onto the Olivier stage at the
National, playing to 1,200 people without a mic.
For that, you've just got to build up your confidence. **Paul McGann**

Remember that you're there to tell the audience a story.

If you fold too much into yourself, you will cease to do this.

There is a very good, very famous note from a director, who said, 'I don't care how you feel – I want to know how you make *me* feel.'

You can tear yourself to bits, but you might not be moving me: in which case, you're failing.

Simon Russell Beale

I've always had very ambitious ideas about acting. I worked in the box office at the National Theatre in Olivier's time, where I saw some very great actors and directors: Maggie Smith, John Gielgud, Paul Scofield. I thought, 'I don't know what the point of being an actor is, unless you're going to be a great actor.' Of course, what I meant by that was a great *theatre* actor. I never thought theatre was a branch of the entertainment industry. I always thought that theatre was an absolutely transformative phenomenon that should be at the heart of community and of society. **Simon Callow**

Make sure you eat before you go on stage. I like to have a salad and a banana at about 6.30 for a 7.30 show. You've got to have your brain working. **Mathew Horne**

You're in trouble when you realise the actor lowers the tone of the set. I've been in productions where the set is so overwhelming that whatever you're doing is irrelevant. If you find yourself in this situation, handle it with good grace. There's not a lot you can do: you've just got to see how you can make it work for you. **Imogen Stubbs**

Theatre is the time for you to really kick things around and get stretched; to see what other people are doing, and really rehearse things. That's where the real work is – and the real fun. **Paul McGann**

You've got to shock the audience sometimes. It can be rather satisfying when you get the slamming of seats, and people walking out. I can remember doing a play at Hampstead Theatre once. I was doing a speech that I thought was really intense and moving – and I saw this man getting up really slowly, gathering his raincoat and all his bits. I didn't even get the impression he was running for a bus. **Jane Asher**

The great thing about the theatre is the environment you're working in. It's full of sweet, silly, ridiculously vain people. But all of them are very human. **Brian Cox**

Nobody's going to give a definitively good performance on the first preview – it happens very occasionally, but that's just a gift from God. The great thing, in my view, is to reach a point where you can say at least one line of your part absolutely in character. Once you feel that, it's a process of just spreading it through the rest of the play. **Simon Callow**

Get lots of sleep. Doing theatre is like doing a night shift, really: you've got to make sure that your body and brain are in peak condition. Don't overfill your days: it's not going to be helpful for the evening. **Mathew Horne**

Always have enough breath to think through to the end of the line. Feel really robust with your breath, your articulation, and your energy. Imagine that you're sending each thought to the back of the theatre – or even up to the heavens. **Samantha Spiro**

A warm-up routine is helpful. I usually do some stretches, some running around to work up my energy, some breathing exercises and some articulation. I prefer to do things in a group with other members of the cast so I feel in touch with their energy for the evening ahead. If you have spent the day in your own little world, it is hard to join forces suddenly when the curtain goes up. For the all-female *Julius Caesar* I was in, we had a ritual that we all did before curtain-up at every single show. It instantly bound us together. **Harriet Walter**

Revel in theatre rituals. Mark press night with cards and flowers. Relish the dinner you're going to have before the show. Take part in warm-ups with the company. Find comfort in all of it: it becomes a form of meditation. **Zawe Ashton**

Your warm-up's very important. Take time to stretch and do voice warm-ups. It helps you focus on the show. **Mathew Horne**

Warm up with the company before you go on stage. Say hello to the theatre. I like to go on stage, stretch my back, loosen my shoulders, and do a few little vocal exercises. **Julie Walters**

Acting for Camera

A successful career in TV or film pays the bills, gets you noticed, and can be very satisfying on an artistic level. But days on set can also be long and tedious, requiring lengthy periods of doing very little – and making a performance to camera look effortless is a lot harder than it seems. Our Players give their tips on how to get it right on camera.

The real art of acting for film and TV lies in preparation. Learn to rehearse your scene in advance, by yourself, so that you know what you want to do with it – but be prepared to turn on a sixpence. Three times out of four, you'll discuss what you want to do with the scene, and the director will buy it. But occasionally, the director will say, 'No, I don't see it like that at all – I don't think you're angry in this scene; I think you keep your cool.' You may have to completely rethink the scene just a few minutes before filming it, and that's quite tricky. I've seen actors come to grief because they've rehearsed a scene another way, and they can't cope. **Oliver Ford Davies**

Play the moment.

Make it look as natural as possible.

One of the things I found most difficult when I first started doing television was that I thought it was like theatre, and I had to project: but you don't.

You're speaking to an audience of one:

>   that person sitting on the sofa, watching the television.

David Harewood

You can't really teach acting for camera. I gather that some drama schools try to – but really, you can only learn how to act in front of a camera by acting in front of a camera. Obviously that's something of a vicious circle because you've got to get the job in the first place. **Mathew Horne**

Don't try to recreate a take. Start afresh. Trying to recreate the same take you just did is like going back to a holiday destination thinking you're going to enjoy it. It's never the same. **Julie Walters**

Know your lines, and don't turn up to the set tired. Just think for a moment about how many thousands of pounds it costs to do a day's filming, even if it's quite low-budget. When the camera turns on you, you are the centre of everything. If you forget your lines, there's nothing anyone else can do about it. They don't want you to be brilliant, they don't want you to be happy: they just want you not to forget your lines. Well, then don't. **Samuel West**

Acting is about energy, and how you control it. This is the major difference between film and theatre. You're still accessing the basic thoughts and feelings, your intentions are still the same – but you have to learn to control your energy in quite different ways. I did a lot of theatre early on, and thought that I knew a lot about theatrical energy, but it took me a long time to understand how to control my energy in front of the camera. **Oliver Ford Davies**

Absorb as much as you possibly can. Filming is not just about you. This is a team, making something, and you are part of that team. I've worked with lots of actors who didn't know what that person over there was doing; who wouldn't even look at them, or learn their names. That's exactly what you shouldn't do. Talk to everyone. Learn where the light's coming from; who you're shadowing; where the camera is. Build relationships with the crew. Don't be afraid to ask what they're doing. They will appreciate it. **Mathew Horne**

Acting for camera is really about *not* acting. A lot of theatre actors fall into a trap of being not altogether truthful because they're having to fill such a huge space. When you're in front of a camera, the opposite is true: if you do too much, it screams down the lens. You need to bring it down, be completely honest, and forget there's a camera stuck up your nose. **Mark Umbers**

A lot can be conveyed in a short clip in close-up. Pretend the camera is your greatest friend, rooting for you. **Harriet Walter**

Keep a buoyancy about what you do – and learn to let go. There are actors who say, 'Can I have another take?' I think sometimes you've just got to allow it to be, and trust that it's going to be right. **Brian Cox**

Remember that the audience is very close, and that you could end up six foot tall on a massive screen. You don't need to project.

It's especially important to remember that if you're coming from theatre.

Julie Walters

The great thing about filming is that it's different every day. If you're there for more than a week, and you get to know everybody, you end up forgetting that the camera's there. That's when the best work happens. **Mark Umbers**

If you have a big film or TV part, you need to stay focused and keep hold of your through-line because the order of scenes is all broken up. People will distract you: sometimes it is very unhelpful to get caught in the chatter. You may be thought aloof and snotty if you keep yourself to yourself – but you have to be prepared for that if it is the only way you will get the job done well. **Harriet Walter**

Draw yourself a mind map. You will usually film out of sequence: you could be doing a bit from the middle first, but you will need to know where you are emotionally for that particular scene. So draw a map of your character's emotional journey. Put in every single thing that happens in the script, and where you are emotionally at that moment: 'We're sixty minutes in, and my mum's just died'; or 'We're seventy-five minutes in, and I've just seen my dog come back to life.' Keep your map on your phone, or print it out and put it on your trailer wall, and you'll always know where you're meant to be on any given day. **Lenny Henry**

Don't get too hung up on the technical aspects of acting for camera. You'll get told where to stand, where to look. Anyone who's employed a young actor before will understand. And there are actors who've been doing it for years and are still crap at standing on a mark. It's good to get good at it: it's helpful for you and the other actors, and it saves time. But nobody at home is going to be watching your feet to see whether you were on your mark. All they're going to be watching is your face. **Luke Treadaway**

I get terrible set fright. Once I did three days at very short notice on *Che*, Steven Soderbergh's film about Che Guevara. I had to learn all this stuff in Spanish when I'd never spoken Spanish before. Then I was suddenly in a jungle, and I had this Steadicam right in my face, with Soderbergh behind it. I was absolutely terrified: I remember I got this twitch in my eye. But I think it was only me who noticed. **Mark Umbers**

Be prepared to do three or four different versions of a take. Don't think your way is the only way. Be open to notes: they might just be leading you in a direction that you don't think will work, but will actually look fantastic on screen. **David Harewood**

Take the pressure off yourself on set. It's all right to make mistakes. It doesn't feel like that at the time – the camera rolls, you become self-aware and your line goes out the window; there are sixty people in the room, and you feel like they're all going, 'Oh for God's sake, all she's got to do is remember the bloody lines.' All you need is one take, and it's fine.

You can't be perfect: luckily, that's why you can do it again.

Jenna Russell

Coping with boredom is a big challenge. You film very little during a filming day: you spend most of it sitting in your Winnebago. Some actors go along to set with books to read and work to do; I tend to just endlessly go over the lines. The worst time was when I played a cameo role in the second *Hobbit* film, and had to wear a huge amount of prosthetics. It took four hours to apply, and changed the shape and size of my head to the extent that I couldn't put on my glasses. I had to sit there reading with a magnifying glass. **Antony Sher**

Be imaginative about how to use the long hours you'll spend sitting around on set. You could do an Open University course; read books and papers; do cryptic crosswords. I can't understand actors who say, 'I'm really bored sitting there all day.' I think, 'Well, do something then.' **Jo Brand**

Not having much to do on a shoot can be tough: you have to remain alert and ready to spring into action though you're spending most of the time waiting around, bored to death, gossiping or doing the crossword. This is a case of learning to manage your energy. No one can really teach you that. Necessity and survival instinct will teach you your own methods. **Harriet Walter**

Take a good book with you. There's a lot of boring time on set. **Helen Baxendale**

Get out of your trailer. Have a look at the set. Ask the sound guy for some headphones; sit by the monitor and watch the other actors. See how they move from one take to the next. Watch how they prepare. Screen acting requires a very different method to stage acting, and the only way you'll learn is by observation. **David Harewood**

Resist the temptation to make other people laugh all the time. You can end up exhausting yourself between takes. **Samantha Spiro**

Film and television directors adore walking scenes, and they are quite difficult. If you're sitting behind a desk, and somebody else is sitting in front of you, there's an obvious difference in status. But in walking along shoulder to shoulder with somebody, that status disappears – you are equivalent. And these scenes are really tricky – there may be people rushing past you; or the director may say, 'When you turn at the bottom into the corridor, you've got to favour the right-hand side because of the lighting.' There's often a great deal to grasp. I remember when I did *Kavanagh QC* with John Thaw, we did all sorts of walking scenes, some of them in a tunnel under Inner Temple. We both sweated over those. **Oliver Ford Davies**

One of the best ways to describe a film set is with the phrase 'Hurry up and wait.' It's not just the actor who has to hurry up and wait: everybody hurries up and waits. So I find film sets very frustrating places to be.

I once did a film in Iceland with a crew of eight – it was wonderful. But if you work on an American movie, the number of people around is just over-whelming. You have to absent yourself from them all just to keep a sense of perspective. **Brian Cox**

Accept that you'll have to do a lot of waiting around. I was once told that a famous actor had had some-body say to him, 'You get a hell of a lot of money doing thirty minutes in a movie.' He said, 'They don't pay me for the acting, they pay me to wait.' That, essentially, is what you're being paid for: to be avail-able at any time. Don't fight against it. **Bill Paterson**

Be protective of yourself when doing screen work. There isn't any aftercare. So much spontaneity will happen on set, and you need to be open to it, but it can be difficult. When I was fourteen, I played a prostitute on drugs: I threw myself into it, but it ended up being much more harrowing than I'd been prepared for. There's nothing wrong with taking yourself out of your comfort zone – but remember that nobody's going to write you a letter afterwards saying you did a great job. **Zawe Ashton**

It's always 50/50: fifty per cent the art and craft of acting – whatever your personal take on that is – and fifty per cent the technical side, which also includes your personal relationships on set. Any shift in that, and something is lost. **Mathew Horne**

Acting Comedy

Delivering any kind of comic script – from an Alan Ayck-bourn farce to one of Shakespeare's comedies – requires a great deal of skill. So is a talent for comedy innate, or can it be learned and refined? Julie Walters, Jo Brand, Lenny Henry, Mathew Horne and Jane Asher – all of whom are renowned, in very different ways, for their skills as comic actors – offer their expert views.

Timing is key to comic acting – and it's a very difficult thing to teach. Some people, like Rowan Atkinson, just have it. You won't know whether you have it or not – so ask other people to tell you.
Jo Brand

There are two different ways of being funny. There's the force-of-nature style, in which you hurl yourself off a cliff and hope something funny happens; and there's the mathematical style, where you break the comedy down into its component parts, and treat it almost like music. I've always gone with the former. If you've been funny since you were little, you will have a general understanding of what's funny and what isn't – even if you're unable to verbalise it.
Lenny Henry

You can't teach anybody to be a comic actor.

You either have it or you don't.

It's about sense of humour; it's an instinct.

Julie Walters

Instinct and fearlessness are key when working on comedy. If someone told me to do stand-up now, there's no way in the world I'd do it. But I embraced that lack of inhibition and freedom at a young age: I went for it, and it paid off. So just give it a go. Make movies on your camera. Do some stand-up. Write sketches and put them on YouTube. Send them to people. I can remember sending some of our sketches to [TV production company] Baby Cow; they weren't used, but at least we got a response. Seven years on, Baby Cow were my executive producers on *Gavin and Stacey*. **Mathew Horne**

Be very careful, when doing a comic play, not to read too much into the atmosphere you're sensing from the audience. If you lose a laugh, carry on as if you've got a laugh. Some audiences are just quieter than others – but they might well be loving it just as much. **Julie Walters**

It's easier to sustain a comedy than a tragedy. It's wonderful to make people cry, or to hear those silences or intakes of breath – but usually it's a bit more traumatic for the actor. With comedy, at least you're getting fed with laughs, and you feel more loved. **Jane Asher**

Farce only works if you play it truthfully.

Make truth your currency.

> To me, the best comic actors are the people who are most truthful: then they can choose whether to over-exaggerate or emphasise something to make you laugh.

Lenny Henry

Perform your own stuff wherever you can. I started off doing a forty-five-minute sketch show with a mate at university, for all our friends. It was only from the success of that that we decided to go out onto the circuit, and try to get five-minute open spots. All my later success as an actor has really come from stand-up. **Mathew Horne**

If you want to do comedy, write it. Write short stories. Try to make your friends laugh. Do amateur dramatics and ask for the funny part. Work out what, and who, makes you laugh. Do you like Peter Sellars or Richard Pryor; Ricky Gervais or Tommy Cooper? Don't copy them, but decide, 'If I'm going to be funny, I want to be as funny as that' – and don't be happy until you are. You won't ever be quite as funny as the person you admire, but there'll be something in between that you'll settle for. **Lenny Henry**

Acting Shakespeare

Any actor whose first language is English – and a good deal of those working in other languages – will tackle Shakespeare at some point. The Players offer their dos and don'ts on bringing the Bard's words to life.

Shakespeare is an incredible language to swim in. Don't be scared of jumping in. Work with a voice coach if you can – it's important to know about rhythms and caesurae, and to understand that iambic pentameter is like a heartbeat. But you can also just read it and jump in. The trick is to not be scared: they're just words. **Lenny Henry**

Trust the writer. Everybody seems to desperately want to jiggle around with him, but as many other people have said – many wiser and better qualified people than me – Shakespeare consists of rhythm and melody. The rhythm is terrifically clearly marked. And to find the melody, think of the text as a song lyric. Just as you wouldn't distort any phrase of the lyric, try to find the shape of the text without distorting any of the lines. **Simon Callow**

The actor's primary responsibility is to make the text understandable at first hearing.

That's quite a big thing, and quite difficult, especially if it's a fairly complicated text.

Know the rules about verse-speaking.

After that, I don't care whether you break those rules – just make me understand what you're saying, the first time you say it.

Simon Russell Beale

Doing Shakespeare is all about clarity and through-line. Every time you say something, it needs to feel like it's the first time you've thought of it. Try speaking the lines very loudly, and then very quietly and intimately. It's a brilliant foundation. **Zawe Ashton**

Go to a part with absolutely no preconceptions. That's more difficult than it sounds, especially with famous parts: if you're doing Iago, you have in your head that he's a psychopath; or that Hamlet is the melancholy prince who can't make up his mind. Read the play like you would if you were analysing it for an essay for an English degree: you'll discover things that take you by surprise. Clear the decks. You'll find it more difficult than you think. **Simon Russell Beale**

Make yourself look an absolute idiot doing facial exercises. Today, in the twenty-first century, we tend to mumble – and with Shakespeare, you're using vocabulary that we just don't use any more. So it's very important that you can get your mouth around the words, and pronounce them. Make sure that you're physically prepared. **David Harewood**

Think of long speeches as a series of connected thoughts, not one big clump of dialogue.

Each thought, each sentence, is a separate piece of your armoury.

Think through each sentence – about how you glue it together; what it means; how you feel when you say each thing. You'll find it comes together like a kind of delicious soup.

Lenny Henry

Cast the audience in a role. I got this from [the director] Roger Michell, years and years ago. So if you're doing Richard III, you're the leader of the gang: you're saying to the audience, 'Look what I can do: I can seduce this woman despite the fact that I've killed her father-in-law and her husband.' If you're Hamlet, you're the loneliest man on the stage, talking to the only friend you have. And if you're Iago, you're lying to the audience; you're saying you don't give a damn what they think. Remember, whenever you have to do a lot of soliloquising, that it's all about what you're telling the audience. **Simon Russell Beale**

Improvising

A few key notes on improvisation, from some of those who really know how to make the method fly.

Improvising is great, but only in very controlled circumstances. I've worked with Mike Leigh a lot. There are a lot of misconceptions about how he works: people think we just turn up on day one and start improvising, but we actually build up our characters over months and months. Otherwise, it's just a load of embarrassed actors standing around, trying to work out the flashiest things to say. **Lesley Manville**

Be prepared to go in unexpected directions. Stay open. Don't block. Pick up on ideas, shapes, movement. Allow yourself to follow and to lead. Don't leave it to the other people in the room to come up with an idea: come up with something yourself. It's very exciting when you work with somebody who's skilled at improvisation: as long as the parameters are right, you can go anywhere. **David Harewood**

Avoid 'competitive' improvisation. This is where everyone is competing to be the most interesting character in the room.

For improvisation to be useful, it needs to be truthful, and you need to observe and listen to the other people in the room just as you have to in real life.

Then you find your moment, say what you want to say, and take up the ringleader role only if it is useful and necessary.

You may have heard other actors saying that listening is the most important thing for an actor: I couldn't agree more.

Harriet Walter

Don't feel, in improvisation, as though you need to be the one who's always doing something. If you trust your fellow actor, and they trust you, things will start to happen for real, and you will both begin to genuinely live in the moment. **Samantha Spiro**

Coping with Stage Fright

Almost every actor experiences some level of nerves before stepping out on stage or facing a film camera. For some, they're the best kind of butterflies, sharpening the mind and the senses. But for others, stage fright can be truly crippling. So what's the best way to handle nerves, and stop them bleeding the joy from the job you love?

You need to be nervous. You'd be the walking dead if you weren't. Acting is a frightening job – stepping out in front of a thousand people and saying 'watch me' for the next two-and-a-half hours. I hate people who call us 'luvvies'. I'd love them to learn Hamlet and then stand next to them backstage waiting to go on for the first time. Then they can talk to me about being a 'luvvy'. **Antony Sher**

Convert fear into excitement.

The physiological symptoms are pretty much the same.

Harriet Walter

Accept that you're going to have nerves to begin with. I don't know many actors who aren't nervous the first time they do a performance on stage. You're nervous about whether you can remember your lines; whether you can get through it; whether the audience are going to like it; whether the other actors are going to remember their lines, or you'll have to bail somebody out. But after that, the nerves should get better. If I continually suffered with agonising, tortuous nerves, I would probably rethink my profession. **Lesley Manville**

Nerves are vanity. Michael Bryant said that to me, and John Gielgud said it to him: it's true, but it's not much help when you're about to go on stage. The most important things are practical: to keep breathing; to plant your feet firmly on the ground and take a deep breath. Just take your time. And remember that nerves are also exciting – perhaps even necessary. **Simon Russell Beale**

Try yoga, breathing exercises and meditation. I have relaxation exercises on my computer: I play them ten minutes before the show to get myself into a place of ease and calm. Knowing your lines thoroughly will help with nerves, too. If you've done your homework, and you've rehearsed, and you've learnt your lines really thoroughly, you won't be nervous. **Lenny Henry**

I love that quote from Judi Dench: she says, 'What right do I have to be nervous?' She does get nervous, as all of us do, but she feels it's quite arrogant and vain — and she's right. When you're nervous, you're worrying what people are going to think of you. Well, actually, that's not your job: the audience aren't there to think about you. They're there to think about the character. **Luke Treadaway**

Never put your stage fright onto anybody else. They're your nerves, and you need to cope with them alone: telling people how you're feeling is just attention-seeking. You are paid to be put under pressure, and to keep that pressure to yourself. Once, just before going on stage, I was so nervous I could hardly breathe. My dresser asked if I was all right, and I said, 'No, I can't do it.' She said, 'There's two thousand friends out there.' Later I told her I was terribly sorry for putting that on her. It's just not fair. **Tracie Bennett**

I think it's rather good to have nerves, especially in theatre. Most people have had them, and they can be crippling: one night you're standing in the wings feeling completely untouchable, and then the very next night you feel like you've never done it before. But nerves do keep you going, especially in a long run, where you can get very tired, and the repetition can drive you slightly crazy. Nerves are a whetstone. **Mark Gatiss**

Performers are like everybody else: we find crowds, and speaking in public, pretty terrifying.

We're just the people who've had a bit of practice, and sort of gotten used to it.

Paul McGann

Stage fright is something that older actors experience more than younger ones. Younger actors can't really afford it. The competition is so hard: if you had yourself as an enemy as well, you'd simply not do it. But I know a lot of older actors who've suffered with it. I sorted mine out with a kill or cure method: doing a one-man show about Primo Levi. It made me realise that my fear was a kind of indulgence, to do with my own ego. Thank God, touch wood, it's gone. **Antony Sher**

Staying Sane
When Things Go Wrong

Forgetting your lines, falling over, discovering that your most important prop is nowhere to be seen… With theatre, the possibilities of things going wrong are endless. So how do you carry on without letting the audience know that things are tumbling around your ears? Should you ever ask for a prompt? And how do you help a fellow actor out of trouble? The Players shed light on how to keep cool in a crisis.

If you forget your lines, try walking around a bit. I tend to do that, or cover my hand with my mouth, or try and make it look like I'm crying. Most of the time you can get away with it in a play, but it's pretty awful if it's during a song. I've known people sing an entire number to 'la la la'. **Jenna Russell**

If you dry, the most important thing is not to panic.
Remember that, in ordinary conversation, you don't ever know what you're going to say next,
> but you always think of something.

The extraordinary thing about plays is that you have to
> pretend to the audience at the beginning of the play that you don't know your lines.

The audience will trust you in that forgetting.

Samuel West

Don't be a perfectionist. This used to be my undoing. I'd think, 'Oh, I've messed up – I might as well write off the whole of tonight's performance.' But missed entrances, mixed-up speeches and forgotten words are all part of the job. In one play, the walls fell down about our ears. If something obvious like that happens, it's best to acknowledge it with some jokey line – like 'The effects of the Central Line', or 'The palace is crumbling, my liege', depending on the period setting. Otherwise, just use lateral thinking to get out of it. Even the most disastrous things going wrong can often go totally unnoticed by the audience. **Harriet Walter**

Listening is key. Knowing the other characters' parts as well as your own will get you through any sticky moments. If you see another member of the company leaving the dressing room without a prop, tell them. You're only ever as good as the other actors. If one of them looks like they don't belong to the world of the play, you will too. **Zawe Ashton**

Everyone will experience lines slipping. You'll either get yourself out of it, or the other actors will help you. Nobody does prompting any more: it's very old-fashioned, and normally the person running the show is no longer sitting in the wings. But yes, things will go wrong. The worst thing that happened to me was snapping my Achilles tendon on stage as the Fool in *King Lear* at the RSC in 1982. I didn't know what had happened at first: I simply found I couldn't stand on one leg. Luckily it happened during the storm scenes, so I could just crawl around until one of the actors lifted me off, and I was rushed to hospital. **Antony Sher**

Help your fellow actor out at all times – but if you go wrong yourself, don't expect them to help you out. I've had things go wrong millions of times. You either forget your song lyrics and have to mime them; or your prop isn't there when it should be. Always get to the theatre early to check the props yourself. Don't leave it to the prop guys. **Tracie Bennett**

Enjoy the things that go wrong. It's these moments of spontaneity and truth that create magic. When something happens on stage that you haven't planned for, you react in that moment both as the character, and as yourself. One of my best moments ever came during a performance of *Gone Too Far* at the Royal Court. I dried, and it seemed to go on for ever – but I found myself circling this one spot on the stage in a very predatory manner. It was exactly right for my angry character, and it got me back. **Zawe Ashton**

Remember that often, no one else knows something has gone wrong. Once, during a performance of *War Horse*, we had a technical malfunction, and the horse didn't come out. I held out my hand as if this was absolutely meant to happen, and went, 'Come on, boy.' It was the longest ten seconds of my life –

another five seconds and I'd have had to start tap-dancing. But eventually they got the thing working. Afterwards, I saw Michael Morpurgo [the writer of the book on which *War Horse* is based] in the bar. He hadn't even noticed. **Luke Treadaway**

The audience very rarely knows that something has gone wrong. It might feel like ten minutes has passed, but it's actually just a moment of madness. The chances are that if you relax, and look into the other actor's eyes, your line will come. If it doesn't, just start speaking rubbish: better to do that than to say nothing at all. **Samantha Spiro**

Forgetting your lines is worse when you're in a musical. I remember Ewan McGregor forgot his lyrics once when we were doing *Guys and Dolls*. He was singing 'I'll Know', and it just went out of his head. He nearly died. He just started singing 'I like to look at your face', over and over again. **Jenna Russell**

Things going wrong makes live theatre fun.

In my days at the RSC, there were some really funny mistakes: people's headdresses catching fire; people forgetting their lines.

Every disastrous show you're in will yield by far the best anecdotes, and possibly the best friends.

Imogen Stubbs

Going the Distance

Most young actors dream of landing that coveted West End role – but performing eight shows a week for up to a year can be a tough slog. Our Players share their wisdom on how to survive long runs.

Understand that every audience is new. Don't rob them of experiencing the play you're in just because you've been doing it for three months and you're sick to the back teeth of it. **Zawe Ashton**

In theatre, the honeymoon period for me is between the first night and four or five weeks in. You're beginning to relax – as long as it hasn't been a total disaster, and there's only two people in the audience. A few weeks later, you go through a period where you think, 'I can't say these things any more – I'm going mad.' Then eventually you come round a bend, and find something you'd never thought of before. **Jane Asher**

You will find a way to get through a long run. *Les Mis* was the first long-running job I ever did: before that, I'd only ever done shows that lasted a week. The idea that I'd still be doing it after three months did my head in. But you just get used to it. It's like going to the gym eight times a week: it's either going to kill you or make you incredibly powerful. **David Thaxton**

It's a sexist thing to say, but I think many women still live a kind of double life during a long run, especially when they have a family. It's very tempting to think, 'I've got all day to do shopping, cooking, fetching from school – maybe do a recording or some radio work, and then do the play in the evening.' I used to do it, but you've got to be pretty fit to make it work. **Jane Asher**

Doing eight shows a week will get you match-fit. Whether it's Shakespeare or a musical or a modern play, by the time you're six weeks into a run, you won't believe that what seemed like such an uphill task when you were rehearsing is now within your body and your bones. **Samantha Spiro**

I like a little variation while I'm performing – not drastic change for its own sake, but I do like slightly changing my moves. Other actors can't bear a fraction of a change. If you stand six inches away from where you usually stand, it throws them. **Jane Asher**

Audiences create their own atmosphere. A few people might start coughing, so then everybody does the same – or someone comes in with a particularly loud laugh, and it liberates the rest of the audience. So don't worry if you feel an audience isn't going where the audience went the night before. You may talk to them afterwards, and realise they've had just as full an experience. **Lesley Manville**

Don't worry if audiences change during a long run. Initially, you get people who are terribly keen; then you get people who've heard it's good; then you get tourists and coach parties. You get different audiences all the time. We always come off and say, 'Ooh, they're a bit boring tonight', or 'They're not really getting it.' But even if you want them to laugh, and they're not laughing, don't cheapen your performance to get a response. You should always perform it exactly as the author wanted it to be. **Jane Asher**

The best trick to rejuvenate your performance in a long run is to listen to the other person. Forget about what you're doing, and just genuinely listen. Almost invariably, your replies will be very slightly different. **Simon Russell Beale**

Alan Ayckbourn is so good at mixing technique with heart and soul. He's often said to me, 'I could find brilliant actors to open one of my plays with no problem at all – it's sustaining it that's the problem.' He's right. You can do it really wonderfully for two or three nights on an immediate emotional high, but it's in sustaining that – appearing to go through the same emotions every night – that technique comes in. **Jane Asher**

TAKING
CRITICISM

Directors: The Good, the So-So, and the Downright Awful

Every actor can remember the best director they've ever worked with — the person who made the whole experience seem so smooth, so effortless. The worst has probably lingered in their memory, too — the one with the stony stare and fork-tongued sarcasm. Most directors probably lie somewhere between the two extremes — but whichever category the director falls into, every actor must find a way to work well with them, and deliver a performance that fits with their vision for the work. Here are some tips from the Players on how to ensure this vitally important relationship stays as happy as it possibly can.

Get over thinking you know best. I've had to learn how to take direction. When I first started acting, I didn't quite know what a director was for: I thought, 'How dare you tell me how to act?' But of course they're not doing that really: they're just trying to take you in certain directions. **Julie Walters**

The right way to take a note is in a way that will increase the amount of love in the room.

Apparently Cyril Cusack used to take notes by writing them down on his copy of *The Guardian*: if he liked it he'd say 'Yes', and if he didn't he'd go 'No'.

Either way, do write them down.

A director should never have to give a note twice.

Samuel West

If you feel uncomfortable saying something, or you don't think your character would say it like that, say so. Only a bad director won't listen to an actor's worries – but, especially when you're starting out, you have to gauge it carefully. Don't be too pushy. **Jane Asher**

Don't be afraid to discuss your director's notes. There should be a climate in the rehearsal room, or set, where the actor isn't just expected to be sycophantic, and say yes to everything. That doesn't mean you should fall out, but constructive debate is a delicious part of the creative process. **Lesley Manville**

Treat your director with deference. I was brought up to call a director 'Sir'. That's no longer usual, but I do feel a great deference to the director, and I think that's right – it's their interpretation you're working on. If you disagree violently, you should say so – but ask if the director would like your opinion before giving it. **Jane Asher**

Don't be afraid to say what you feel about the part, or that you feel you're being pushed in the wrong direction. I've seen young actors struggling because they're with a powerful director and he's giving them notes they don't understand. Collar the director; make him do his job. Don't struggle on and then get to a first night and think, 'I don't know what I'm doing.' **Julie Walters**

Do what the director says. It's that simple. It gets difficult if you clash with the director over where you think your character's going, and what you think is required. There's no set way of sorting that out: you just have to work it out as you go. But don't bitch about it. Don't be that guy. No one likes him. **David Thaxton**

I like directors, but their importance is slightly overblown. Say to the director, 'Okay, yes, fine', and then get on and do it. There's no good stamping your feet and saying, 'I don't think that's right.' I've always managed to get the best out of everybody by not questioning too much: by just saying, 'We're all in the same boat: let's get on and do it.' **Brian Cox**

The director is the captain of the ship. At times you'll feel you have the most amazing leader, both as a person and as an artist. But not everyone's like that. I've worked with directors who aren't natural leaders, and only want the lines said their way, with their interpretation, and even the same pitch and rhythm. You think, 'Okay, this is going to be a long five weeks.' **Luke Treadaway**

Take notes not just graciously, but gratefully. Don't argue back.

You get actors who, as soon as a director starts to give a note, will say, 'Ah, what I was trying to do...'

What you were trying to do is irrelevant – just listen to what the director, if it's a good director, is saying, because it's worth gold.

I love notes; I thrive on them. I can't wait for someone to help me go further than I can by myself.

Antony Sher

The best directors are enablers: they direct you without you even realising it. Howard Davies has a gentle, encouraging quality, which makes you feel good about what you're trying to do. Directors who don't get it right are very prescriptive about what they're after. Ideally, you will find your way in to what they want. But don't be afraid to surprise them. **Mark Gatiss**

There are unhelpful directors out there. David Suchet says that when an actor first stands up [in rehearsal], he or she is a tiny little lighter flame, walking around, going, 'I don't know why I'm here.' The director can come in with one note and blow out the performance. So the director should be very gentle. But as an actor, don't push yourself towards a result. Keep in mind that what you're doing is a process. **Samuel West**

Honesty is usually the best thing. If something really isn't suiting you, you should bring it up. I worked with two other actors way back in the sixties; recently, I met someone who directed us, and he said that one of the things that made us special was that we were completely open about our criticism of each other without ever losing our friendship. Be prepared to bring things up to both actors and directors. Don't hide it away and nurture a grievance. **Bill Paterson**

Pick your battles.

Don't fight to the death because you don't think your character would wear this particular jumper.

Luke Treadaway

Eight out of ten times, you will trust your director, and go on a journey with them. Try everything; be open. But don't exhaust yourself trying everything with a director you just don't agree with. Nod, smile and show willing; save your energy and work it out for yourself. There's no point in being argumentative: it wastes too much time. **Samantha Spiro**

Don't be afraid to say, 'I don't know how to act this.' I've said that a few times over the past few years. I'd never have said that as a young person – I'd have agonised over it. I'd have felt it meant I wasn't a good actor. But it doesn't mean that at all. **Julie Walters**

Some directors are very strict. Michael Grandage is of the mind that you turn up ten minutes before rehearsals to say your hellos, and when you're in the room you're in the room, you're not sitting looking at the *Evening Standard*. I think there's something quite wonderful about that: your time in the room is concentrated. **Jenna Russell**

Always hold on to a bit of self-protection. You have to 'own' your performance in the end, but too much defensiveness can deafen you to useful criticism. Listen to everything, try everything, and only if and when you are convinced the director is wrong, then quietly get on with how you wanted to do it in the first place. They probably won't notice, and may say it was all their idea. **Harriet Walter**

Cruelty is unforgivable – however great the director is. I think it's lovely when young actors express their opinions. But I remember one rehearsal, where one of the understudies was sitting observing what we were doing, and piped up with something I thought was good. The director looked at him like death and said, 'If I want your opinion, I'll ask for it.' And he was just crushed. **Jane Asher**

Keep your mind alert to your own taste. It's very undermining for a director if you immediately challenge and contradict them. Always try what the director's asking for. But you equally have a right to say, 'I don't think it's working, can I try something else?' If you don't do what's at the back of your head, it tends to come out in your performance anyway, as an act of rebellion. **Imogen Stubbs**

Try not to be defensive with a director. If there's something you fundamentally disagree with, it's going to be difficult; but nine times out of ten, the person who's watching may not be getting what they want. Trust your director. You might think you're doing what is required, but it might not be coming across. **David Harewood**

Listen to the director and translate what they've said into your own head.

See what positive things can be gained by trying out their note.

And sometimes, just say 'Yes' and then do it how you want.

Luke Treadaway

Most directors are infinitely better if you give them the benefit of the doubt. Being a director is very nerve-racking. On the whole, if you go with them, they will be the best that they can be. Nobody wins when a company undermines the director. The whole thing falls down the plughole: all the actors are directing each other and it becomes a mess. **Imogen Stubbs**

Some directors love a lot of input. Rufus Norris is the epitome of collective rehearsals: he's so open to people suggesting things, trying things out. I loved working with him. But some directors can take it too far, and be so collaborative that you feel they're not actually doing anything at all. You want to feel you've got somebody at the helm. **Jane Asher**

You may find yourself working with a director whose approach is anathema to you. Figure out how you're going to handle that. You can go along with it as far as you can – but at the same time, keep your own counsel and know the work you have to do on yourself. Remember that the director may be deliberately trying to push you away from what you normally feel comfortable with. And that can be a very valuable thing indeed. **Simon Callow**

Some actors don't like doing their homework. When I'm directing, I try not to employ those actors – but there are some who will get nervous with too much homework. It's up to the director to keep these actors feeling like they're on the right path. Actors think they want to be safe but they don't: they want to be dangerous in a safe way. **Samuel West**

One of the most exciting experiences I had was when I took on a job I didn't particularly want to do. It was with a young first-time film director. I said, 'Okay, look, I'll do the role, but I'm just going to turn up; you tell me what to do, and I'll do whatever you say.' I had no opinion about what I was doing, and it was one of the most liberating things I'd ever done. I wasn't letting my own opinions get in the way. **Brian Cox**

Treat directors (and writers) as innocent until proven guilty. The good ones, if you don't resist them, will take you places you never thought you could reach. **Harriet Walter**

Reviews:
Friend or Foe?

You spend weeks rehearsing, dredging your heart and soul to bring your character to life – and then the critic walks in and grades your performance with a great big cross or tick. That's how it can feel to the actor anyway. But a good critic can provide a vital external perspective on your acting, and at best bring a dimension to the work that you hadn't previously noted. However, it's one thing reading reviews of a film you made a year ago, and quite another checking Twitter every five minutes to see what the critics have said about the performance you've got to keep on giving for the next three months. So is it advisable to read your reviews – and if so, when? Our Players offer their guidance.

Reading reviews has to be a personal choice. I do read them, with a view to learn. Reviewing is an art-form in itself, and it's good to know that what you're doing is either effective or ineffective. But you have to filter out the things that are personal, or consider that there may be another agenda. Remember that reviewers are the only people who aren't reviewed.
Mathew Horne

Print out the speech by Theodore Roosevelt that starts 'It's not the critic that counts', and stick it on the wall next to your bed.

It expresses exactly what actors need to think.

What really matters is the person who dares to stand up and do something in the first place.

You might fail, and fail miserably, but you *did* dare:

and that's worth something.

Imogen Stubbs

Don't read your reviews – especially not the bad ones. Remember that you've got to go on every night and face an audience. It's nice to hear that the reviews are generally good. But even reading fantastic things about yourself makes you self-conscious. **Julie Walters**

Sometimes it works and sometimes it doesn't: you have to just breathe and go, 'Well, there we are.' You can't please everybody. **Jenna Russell**

The thing about reviews is, if they say you're a genius, and you believe it, what happens when the same person says you're shit? You've got to believe that too. So it's probably best not to read any of them. If you're in a play, you'll know what's being said anyway: your friends will have that face on after the first night. **Lenny Henry**

You'll never learn anything from a review. There are great critics who understand what I do, and I respect them. But I don't allow myself to really believe what they say. You're not doing it for reviews: it's not about the afterwards or the before. It's about the moment, and the unique experience of that moment, with that audience, in that theatre. **Brian Cox**

Professional critics are, on the whole, not the best people to judge acting. Pick two or three people whose judgement you rely on and listen to them. But try to develop your own inner critic who is honest, but not too discouraging. That's the most reliable in the end.

Harriet Walter

I gave up reading reviews thirty years ago. Good reviews can be as unhelpful to an actor as bad ones. The moment a critic has said, 'And when he did "To be or not to be", I felt shivers down my spine', the actor will never be able to make anyone's spine shiver again. But you'll find out what the gist of the reviews is anyway. If the reviews are bad and the play's in the West End, you'll probably be taken off, and thus be put out of your misery. **Antony Sher**

Reviews are a tricky thing. As actors, we're here to please and to entertain the audience, whether we choose to admit this or not. So you naturally want to know what critics are thinking: it's not about wanting to be liked, but about whether you're on the right track. But it's very difficult to get a clear picture. One of the first shows I did was *Educating Rita*, when I was twenty-one. Everybody was talking about the reviews. I read one, and it was embarrassingly brilliant; but the next one said I was the worst thing they'd ever seen. I stood there at stage door, thinking, 'I don't know who to believe.' So from then on I decided I would only listen to myself, the director, and the writer. **Tracie Bennett**

With every other job I do, I say, 'This time, you're not going to read the reviews.' But I always do. It's that feeling that people are talking about you behind your back: you want to know what's being said. **Mark Umbers**

A big motto of mine, especially doing stage work, is

'Cancel and continue.'

You can't get everything right. No one's really judging you.

Jenna Russell

The press can be very unpleasant. They're often strange: even if they like you, you should be worried. You want to be able to respect them and learn from their reviews, and occasionally you can. But sometimes they're just so unnecessarily brutal and damning. It's like a gladiatorial match: either amazing, five stars, or terrible, one star. Most things are somewhere in between. **Imogen Stubbs**

Reviews are none of your business. The good ones make you smug and the bad ones make you depressed. The director should read them, and if there's anything useful in them, pass it on in a useful way. And avoid pillow-talk notes. I have a little card with my mobile number on; when I'm directing, I give it out to the actors during previews and say, 'If you have loved ones in, with suggestions, please get them to call me.' **Samuel West**

It's better not to read your reviews. You don't want to be picking out anything particular in your performance: you just want to be playing it. And if they pick out a good bit, you can bet your bottom dollar it won't be any good next time because you'll be thinking about how good it is. **Helen Baxendale**

The desire to read reviews is a bit like a fever: when press night happens and the reviews come out, you can't think about anything else. But if you leave it about a week, it goes away. **Mark Gatiss**

'Reputation is Everything': How to Ensure Yours Stays Good

Actors like to talk. So do directors, playwrights, agents, stage managers, gaffers and the people who make the tea. Treat any of them with arrogance or disdain, and news of your bad attitude will quickly spread around the industry. Treat all of them with respect, and they'll respect you in return – and you'll all have a much nicer time. Sounds simple, right? Well, yes, it should be. Here, our Players reflect on how to ensure your reputation never starts working against you.

Reputation is everything. How you behave in a rehearsal room; how you behave on a set; how you treat your dressers; how you speak to your driver in the morning: all these things do come back and bite you on the bum if you misbehave. I know of a really big director who will ring up at least three other people in different areas – another director; maybe somebody who was on the stage door – before he employs somebody he's not worked with before to find out if they're a good person. **Jenna Russell**

Don't keep people waiting.

Julie Walters

Don't be so screamingly overambitious that it veers into looking ugly and unattractive. That kind of pushiness is a turn-off. **Lesley Manville**

There's nothing more unattractive than ambition, but there's nothing as attractive as conscientiousness. There's an urban myth that crews hate actors. It's not true. Crews generally love actors, otherwise they wouldn't do that job. But if you go in as an ambitious starlet, ignoring everyone, making everything about you, they won't like you. Go in and just try to do a really good job, and you will gain some respect. And they will help you: you've got to remember that there are people around, like best boys, who can make you look like shit on camera. I've seen it happen. It's about mutual accommodation. **Mathew Horne**

I can't bear young actors – or anybody – who are so full of themselves, they don't feel they have to put any work in. But that happens very rarely. **Lesley Manville**

Keep the atmosphere good. I like a happy set where people can have a laugh. I get to know the crew, chat with them. I think that's very important. Creating an atmosphere where other people are frightened to tread is, I think, really unprofessional. There are people who do that, and make it very difficult for other people to do their jobs. But all the jobs on a film set are important, no matter what they are. **Julie Walters**

Be kind.

There is a persistent and stupid idea that you have to have a miserable time to create great art.

That's nonsense.

It will always be hard work: there's never enough time or enough money; tempers fray; you have to concentrate.

But ultimately it should be fun – and the best way of ensuring that is to be kind to each other.

It's so simple, and yet it's remarkable how few people get it.

Mark Gatiss

My friend John Castle says the best advice for any actor is written on the door at RADA: 'Push.' But remember the difference between pushing and being pushy. There's nothing wrong with ambition and setting your sights high – but how you do it is the difference between a good actor and a great actor. I can't tell you how off-putting it is to be cornered by someone telling you how brilliant they are. **Mark Gatiss**

Your reputation will precede you. Be nice to people on the way up. I heard a great story once. There were two sparks [lighting technicians on set] who really bullied this young runner. About a year later, he came on set and the same sparks were there. They started on him; told him to get them a tea. He said, 'No, you get your own tea – and you're fired. I'm the producer.' That's how quickly things turn around in TV. You have to be very aware of that. **Mathew Horne**

I have worked with some young actors – and older ones – who are very obvious about who they're nice to. I've seen them be shockingly awful to people when they think they can get away with it. No, no, no. The resident director who comes in and gives you notes could be running the Royal Court in ten years' time. Everyone's there to do a job; they're not there to service you. A bit of respect for everybody goes a long way. **Jenna Russell**

Understand the difference between concentration and pretension. I have no patience at all with actors who will only be addressed by their character name. If you're about to go on stage or set and you're playing a paraplegic with an Irish accent, I can understand why you might want to get yourself into the character, and not talk about the football results. But if you insist on being addressed by your character name when you're in the canteen, then you're a wanker. **Mark Gatiss**

Be careful with vanity and ego. These are the traps that actors have. Learn to have fewer opinions about yourself and the work. Keep an open mind about everything. As you get older, you realise that the more you know, the less you know – and that feeds into the work as well. **Brian Cox**

There's a fine line between persistence and toadying – and it's what makes the difference between people who get on, and people who don't. **Mark Gatiss**

I have worked with idiots, both actors and directors. One of them was an actor who refused to do the off-lines with me – that's when you do a scene in a film with another actor: you're on camera, and the other actor is off-camera. I just said to the director, 'Oh, I'm so relieved. I would only find it a distraction.' I just thought, here is a guy who isn't behaving properly. **Brian Cox**

Never be more interesting in the bar than you are on stage. A director once told me that.

Don't ever feel that your personality has to be the most attractive thing about you as an artist. You need to save your energy for the work: the banter isn't that important.

Zawe Ashton

Don't put photographs of your fellow cast members on Facebook or Twitter without their permission – and be very wary about tweeting any details about the production. A lot of older actors feel, quite rightly, that it's an invasion of privacy. Be careful about what you put out in the public domain. **Jenna Russell**

Be very careful when using social media. Don't upset anyone you're working with, or tweet spoilers about the show or programme you're in. Be aware that not everybody who follows you has your best interests at heart. **David Harewood**

Think carefully about whether to be on Twitter. I'm on it because I'm a curious person: I like to know what's going on. But I believe that if you're an actor, you're paid to convince people that you're someone you're not. That's the bottom line. On those grounds, it helps if people don't really know anything about you. **Mark Umbers**

Don't search your name on Twitter. I did that a couple of years ago, and I don't do it any more. Apparently I should be hanged. **Mathew Horne**

A Few Words on Fame

The vast majority of actors go about their business without being bothered by fans in the street. But land that major TV part or big film role, and you might soon catch people staring, or find strangers discussing the shape of your ears on the internet. So how do you cope with the fact that all these people you don't know suddenly know you? Here is some advice from the Players who've been there, done that, and realised that fame isn't all it's cracked up to be.

Nobody can describe to you what fame feels like. You walk onto a train or into a restaurant, and people have a preconception about you. You see them whispering, nudging, sneakily taking photographs. It's utterly terrifying, and you are never warned about quite how difficult it is. It changes your whole sense of who you are in the world. I don't think I'm built for it. When it happened to me, I became a bit of a recluse. **Mathew Horne**

Some people take fame and grasp it, love it, embrace it. I didn't enjoy it at all. I'm much happier now, with people only thinking they know me from some party. Anonymity is a wonderful, valuable thing. **Helen Baxendale**

Just keep your head down and do the best you can. Don't get caught up in the hype. My first proper TV job was a show called *20 Things to Do Before You're 30* on Channel 4. It was thirteen one-hour episodes, and I was one of four leads. I was twenty-three: it was a huge break. The producers were going, 'This is going to be massive', and I went into full excitement mode. I ran and swam every day to lose weight. I rang my mum saying, 'I'm on a billboard.' And it flopped big time – which was devastating, but also a brilliant lesson. **Mathew Horne**

Preserve your mystery as much as you can. There's a reason why actors used to leave the stage door with a cloak over their face: the more your baggage is laid out in front of the public, the more restricted you are in terms of the characters you can play. Young actors today are likely to be impaled on publicity early on, so you need to be very brave from the beginning. Say, 'I am going to commit one hundred per cent to my acting, but I am not a publicity machine.' That is probably going to lose you some jobs – but the alternative is far worse. **Imogen Stubbs**

Being an actor is a constant learning process: it's very much a marathon and not a sprint. You may have recognition now, but unless you get hit by a bus, fingers crossed you'll be doing it until you drop dead of natural causes. Fame is very transient: the media knock you down and build you up. So see your career as a long-term thing. **Mathew Horne**

Fame and fortune are by-products of this profession that come to very few. Those things can't be your main aim. In any case, rejection and failure teach you far more than success. If you aim to be in it for life, enjoy just doing it; enjoy collaborating with other creative people. That allows you to achieve more than the sum of the parts – and it is a better formula for the long haul. **Harriet Walter**

KEEPING
GOING

Day Jobs:
How to Make Ends Meet
without Losing Hope

News flash: acting, like the rest of the arts, is extremely badly paid. Yes, there's the one per cent who make it to Hollywood and command $10m a film. But for the other ninety-nine per cent, making ends meet is often a matter of cobbling together theatre, film and telly work with adverts, voice-overs, or another day job that keeps body and soul together while leaving your mind free to prepare for your next audition. Here are a few words on how to keep a roof over your head when acting alone isn't paying the bills.

It's in the downtimes that you really learn about yourself. Stay open in those dark days. Don't feel as if waiting tables is beneath you; don't feel ashamed to take a menial job. You've got to do what you've got to do to put food on the table. Put your pride to one side, and make sure you can just get through and keep yourself sane. You'll thank yourself further down the line: you'll think, 'I'm glad I did that just to survive: now I get to do what I want to do, which is act.' **David Harewood**

If you need to take on other work, look for something that involves communicating with people –

    working in a bar or club; tour guiding; teaching; counselling –

rather than something that ties you to an office in a rather solitary job.

It may be easy and comfortable to find a protective shell, but it makes things difficult when you're suddenly called to be extrovert again with your next acting job.

Harriet Walter

Have something else you can do. Living on acting alone is so risky – you're going to need something else. Most actors will be working in cafés or somewhere, and that's fine. **Jane Asher**

The main day job I did was as a legal proofreader at a law firm in the City. It was about four hours a day: enough to just get by, but it meant I always had time in the morning or afternoon to do an audition if it came up. **Mark Umbers**

Find a way to make it work financially. I get kids writing to me all the time asking if I can give them the money for next year's drama-school fees. I understand the difficulty they have today because fees are so high and there are no grants, but it was a struggle even in my day. At Italia Conti, we were all working from 4 p.m. till midnight, every single night. Working in supermarkets, waitressing; my friend was a Greek dancer. We look back and say, 'How did we do that?' But we were hard workers, and we were hungry. **Tracie Bennett**

I did quite a few different jobs. I worked down the Portobello Road [in London], on the market, which I loved – but I definitely didn't feel like an actress. And I worked in Gap, which wasn't so great. Some people find working in theatre very successful, in something other than acting: dressing, or doing front-of-house. But I never wanted that: it would have made me too hungry inside to be acting. **Samantha Spiro**

There's nothing wrong with taking other jobs outside acting:

you have to keep body and soul together.

But don't let yourself get too easily sidetracked.

You don't want to find, in five years' time, that you're a manager at John Lewis, and not an actor any more.

Mark Gatiss

Exercising
Body and Mind

If you're lucky, an acting career is a marathon, not a sprint. Here's how to ensure you stay fighting fit, both on and off stage.

Prepare for a show as a sportsman would for a big event. As a kid, I was a track and field athlete – a triple jumper. I was good at it, and I've never really shaken off my attachment to sport. The times I've stood in the wings, waiting to go on, trying to focus: it's the same buzz that you see with athletes on TV, waiting to go down the track. So my preparation is a sporting preparation. I eat well, I get fit. I save my energy for the show in the evening. I read that Mark Rylance did almost five hundred performances of *Jerusalem.* You can't do a run like that without getting in shape. **Paul McGann**

It seems to me that the key to everything, whether it's acting or dancing or kung fu, is relaxation. Learn to relax. Seek out a guru or a mentor. A director doesn't want to see you hyperventilating on the floor before rehearsals. **Lenny Henry**

Take lots of vitamins, and don't go mental on the set catering.

You wouldn't eat a roast dinner followed by jam roly poly at home on a Monday lunchtime – so don't eat it on set.

Jo Brand

Keep fit. Being on stage takes a lot out of you – the projecting, the gearing yourself up and doing it, is exhausting. I feel better on stage if I'm reasonably fit. You have to keep the instrument going: it's all you've got to work with. **Jane Asher**

Don't feel guilty about slobbing around when you're not working. Relax, put your pyjamas on, watch shit TV. Empty your mind. **Tracie Bennett**

When you're not working, try to do everything to keep yourself stimulated. Keep your body in good shape. Keep reading interesting novels. Go and see films. Sign up for all the theatres where you can get cheap seats. If you haven't got an agent, work hard to try to get yourself one. If you've got an agent, work hard to keep them interested in you. Keep your antennae working at all times. **Lesley Manville**

Sleep well, drink lots of water, eat all the good food you can afford. It doesn't have to be expensive: I lived on thirty-nine-pence-a-pound turkey drum-sticks and cabbage for three years. It's a kind of science: you have to learn a routine with your body. If you eat too late, for instance, you might feel like vomiting on stage; but if you eat too early, your brain can't function. And don't drink Coke at the half. I did that once, and I was burping all the way through the performance. **Tracie Bennett**

Recognise fatigue and low resistance when it hits you.

Eat properly: no rich food late at night because you need to sleep properly.

But don't fret if you can't manage these – fretting is a great wearer-down. (I do not practise what I preach here.)

Harriet Walter

If you're really serious about acting as a career or a passion, you have to keep trying to develop your techniques and your craft; keep on looking for ways to improve. Footballers don't join a football club at sixteen and then just play every week; those footballers keep working with different nutritionists, coaches, managers. And most actors don't even have the luxury of playing every week. **Luke Treadaway**

Look after your health. Keep other interests going. Get a sense of proportion by looking beyond your world and seeing how relatively lucky you are. Be open to new people and new influences. Welcome the fact that this job can throw you together with all age groups and types, and allow yourself to be stimulated by them. **Harriet Walter**

Keep fit. Pilates works well for me because it's about strength and feeling fluid and flexible. Keeping your mind fit is also important – as is drinking lots of water and trying not to drink too much booze. Though of course one drink is always very good after a show: especially on press night. **Samantha Spiro**

Go and see plays and movies. Read often. And if you want to take a class, go take a class. Learn how to get yourself into a zone of positivity, so that when you're next going for an audition, you're not going, 'Fuck, it's going to be awful.' You're going, 'I'm in a zone. I'm cool.' **Lenny Henry**

Surviving the Tough Times

...And there will be tough times. Losing out on parts, writing endless unanswered letters to agents, not getting an audition for months on end: even the most committed actors can get down at times. Here's how to keep the faith in the face of even the toughest setbacks.

Don't sit at home watching afternoon TV. It's fine to do that for an hour or so, but to give into that kind of lifestyle is not helpful. You've got to keep the faith and keep going. Keep doing your auditions, turning up on time, being a good worker. Hopefully something will crack, and there'll be an opening. **Lesley Manville**

Don't worry about empty theatres. There will be times when one is in a play that just doesn't work, and one is lumbered with just carrying on. **Jane Asher**

Being unemployed is part of the job. Often agents will say you need to be unemployed in order to get work. If you don't get something you really wanted, a month later you might be doing something else that alters things in a positive way. Your time will come. **Jenna Russell**

There will always be somebody who's not as good at what you do as you are,
	and there will always be
	somebody who's better.
Kathy Burke told me that.

It's the one thing that has always kept my feet on the ground.

Mathew Horne

Do things for the right reasons, and something will always turn up. Do everything from a true, loving place, and be ready and primed to work. **Tracie Bennett**

Go and see other people working, even when you're not. It may be difficult, but it will keep you connected. **Bill Paterson**

Being away from loved ones can be tough. But it can actually strengthen a relationship, especially if you're both doing what you want to do, and you appreciate that in each other. It might not be the best-paid job, but you're doing something that is satisfying your soul. **Samantha Spiro**

Find ways to fill your time when a job finishes. I always start writing something the second I finish a job: a screenplay or an adaptation of a novel. For me, that serves half as a holiday, and half as a way of keeping my brain in gear. **Mark Umbers**

Take up cricket and golf. Do useful things to get through the tough times. **Bill Paterson**

If I'm not working, I tell myself it's because I'm tired and I've chosen not to. Clear out your house; do your paperwork. See old friends. Go to the theatre. Save for that rainy day. Budget. Catch up with life. Go out and let your hair down. **Tracie Bennett**

It won't work if you're too
needy.
You've got to hold on
tightly, and let go
lightly.

T.S. Eliot says it better:
'Teach us to care, and
not to care.'

Perform a balancing act
between the two extremes.

Brian Cox

Spend time reading plays and screenplays when you're not working. Everything's so accessible these days. If you can find your way round a screenplay, or another director's working methods, it could stand you in good stead when you get the next job. **Mark Gatiss**

The only really wonderful bits about the acting profession are when the script thuds through the letterbox onto the doormat (or that email pings into your inbox with an attachment); and when your agent rings and says, 'Darling, it's an offer.' From then on, it's downhill. The rehearsal is agony; the first night is terrifying; and then you get the boredom of being in a run. (I'm half-joking, of course. But you do have to try to keep it fresh.) **Jane Asher**

Making Time for a Life Beyond Acting

Yes, that's right: there is more to life than acting, however much it means to you. And your friends, family and interests outside the profession are what keep you going when your agent hasn't called for weeks on end. Our Players reflect on how to ensure you don't make acting the only thing that matters.

Don't let it all be about your career. It's such a thin existence, in the end. **Julie Walters**

See acting as a job. It's a job you love, but it's still a job; otherwise you end up putting far too much pressure on yourself. **Jenna Russell**

There will be times when the work has to come first, even when it gets in the way of your relationships. Sometimes it's horrible. I can remember disappearing when my children were little: on the day they broke up from school in the summer, I had to go to South Africa, and the day they returned was the week I came back. It hurt – but if the family always comes first, then you might not eat. **Paul McGann**

Have something else in your life.

It's a fickle profession, and if it's your only passion it can leave you very empty.

Don't make it the be-all and end-all.

Helen Baxendale

Have a life outside the industry.
Make time for friends and
relationships outside the
job.
Have family time; relationship
time; travel time.

You live in your own head a lot
in this industry.
There's always
something to be said
for stepping out of
it.

Zawe Ashton

The other people in your immediately dependant family *must* be more important than your work. I wasn't sure I could commit to that, so I opted not to have children. My husband is an actor and we understand the demands of the profession; that makes it easier. **Harriet Walter**

Make a decision about whether you're prepared to be away for long periods. As soon as I had a child, I cut out weekends and summer holidays and Christmas. I've never been away for more than two weeks at a time. I couldn't go away for months: you may as well live on the moon. **Julie Walters**

You're very fortunate that you're only working four hours a day, but they happen to be the least sociable hours imaginable. You've just got to deal with that. Accept that if you've got lots of friends outside the industry, you're only going to see them on Sundays. You can see why so many actors get together. If you're in a show with someone, you have the 'show bubble': it's the only thing in your life, and it's not very healthy, but I can see why it happens. **David Thaxton**

The nature of the job is that it takes over everything. Friends and partners have to be incredibly understanding and know what they're getting into. If you're a theatre actor, you just don't have a social life other than with the people you're working with. I often think, because of that, you get a completely different breed of person within the industry. People tend not to have social lives, so they just keep working and working. **Mark Umbers**

Maintain your out-of-work friendships. On a set, the actors and crew become your family, your friends. It was particularly like that when we filmed *Gavin and Stacey* out in Cardiff. Film sets are like playgrounds: there's flirting and relationships and gossip and bitching; lots of sex and laughter. It's really fun, but it can give you a false sense of reality. Your heart can deceive you at times. **Mathew Horne**

Tell your friends to be brutally honest with you. **Jo Brand**

If you want to write as well as act, do it. Ignore the voice over your shoulder saying you can't. There's a British disease: people mistrust you if you do more than one thing. But as a writer as well as a performer, I don't have to wait for the phone to ring. I create my own work. **Mark Gatiss**

Don't mind too much in the end. The last thing you want to do is choose a career that ruins your life. Have other loves. And when you do get work, treat it as a great joy. **Helen Baxendale**

Have other interests. Hang out with people who aren't actors. Take your head out of it, and find other things that make you happy. If you become too obsessed with acting, and you're not doing it, you're going to go mental. **David Thaxton**

Staying Inspired

We've heard all about rejection, and nasty reviews, and the difficulties of making ends meet. But none of that will deter the actor who truly loves this restless, fascinating, constantly evolving art form. Here are some words of encouragement from the Players to keep that light of inspiration burning.

Keeping going should be the sum of your ambition. I remember sitting at RADA in the common room with Kenneth Branagh and Mark Rylance: all these theatre stars, sitting round one morning going, 'Sod this for a lark – I want to be a movie star.' By the time I was twenty-six, I got into a movie, and that was it – everything else has been a bonus. If your only ambition is to keep going, that really should be it. They're never going to tell you to retire. **Paul McGann**

If you're working, that is success. Obviously it's lovely to get really fantastic jobs, but the very fact that you're managing to live and do the job that you want to do is a success in itself. **Jenna Russell**

Acting is the best job in the world.

It's miserable, and horrible, and eighty per cent of actors are out of work.

But it's also endlessly fascinating, and diverse, and without it, I would never have known about string theory, or currency exchange speculation, or Alzheimer's.

And even if eighty per cent of actors might be out of work, that means that twenty per cent are in work.

Simon Russell Beale

Blame is a waste of time in this profession. Shit happens. It is one of the least fair professions in the world. Bitterness and blame will only make the shit that happens shitter. **Harriet Walter**

Look after your enthusiasm, because it will be tested. Try to enjoy the simple things. Actors are easy to lampoon, but they are some of the best people I've ever met. They're well-adjusted. They're spirited. They're good workers: if things are going well, they'll stay till it's dark. They're right behind you. **Paul McGann**

If you want longevity, you've got to play the long game: behave like a decent human being, and have a good time. **Jenna Russell**

Keep the faith by getting work. It's particularly tricky for women as we get older: there are fewer female parts to begin with, and then as you hit a certain age there are even fewer. So just try to enjoy the work that you do get. **Helen Baxendale**

Make sure acting is the job you really chose. I've been doing it for thirty years, and there have been times when it's been really nerve-racking – when I've only just kept the wolf from the door. In those times, the great consolation has to be that it's the thing you chose. If it's what you chose to do, you'll take the bad times. There's nothing better than to end up doing the thing that you wanted to do. It will keep you happy; it will keep you alive. **Paul McGann**

Avoid negative people.

It's very easy to be around other actors who moan all the time – about money, about not getting a part, about directors. My old manager used to call it 'locker-room talk'. Just don't be around those people.

Lenny Henry

Avoid bitterness. It's easy to fall prey to a bitter feeling; to think, 'I'm playing this part, but why aren't I playing that part?' This applies way up the hierarchy: I've seen it, and it's very corrosive. I don't mean that you have to sit back and be happy with where you are. You need to stay determined and ambitious – but bitterness is bad. **Oliver Ford Davies**

Acting is a thing that doesn't leave you. People become actors and then get disappointed and stop doing it. But it never leaves you: it's part of your vocation. You might sometimes be thwarted: you might see careers and think, 'They didn't get what they deserved.' But that's life: that's the way it goes. Then you see people get what they deserve: after forty years, they emerge into the actors you always knew they were. And that's the really exciting thing about it. **Brian Cox**

Keep at it. Even Judi Dench and Ian McKellen didn't start playing leads in films until quite late in their careers. **Oliver Ford Davies**

Success in acting is hugely down to luck, and having a sense of purpose. Woody Allen said ninety per cent of success is turning up. **Mark Gatiss**

Time travel is one of the wonderful pluses of this business. Recently, I went from playing economist Adam Smith on stage at the Royal Court, to re-enacting the negotiations that led to the First World

War for a film. There we all were, sitting round the Cabinet table for three weeks, saying, 'Isn't it incredible to relive this, almost verbatim?' What other job allows you to travel back in time? **Bill Paterson**

You'll get all kinds of advice about what you should do. I'm doing it now. But to me, the main thing is just persistence. It really is. It's remarkable the number of people you'll meet in a room at a party who'll moan about their lost chances, and you'll think, they didn't *really* stick at it. Really, it's a combination of persistence and luck. **Mark Gatiss**

It's a very privileged job: there's no other like it. It's given me insights that a life as a coal miner might never have led to. **Brian Cox**

Try to vary what you do as much as possible. Sometimes you don't know which area suits you, where you excel. Sometimes it's the most surprising thing that makes you go, 'I really, really enjoyed that.' **Jenna Russell**

Have unwavering faith.
Not necessarily in your own
abilities –
although that counts –
but just be completely
dogged about not giving up.

If you're on the dole, like I was, and you have no money, and everybody's crying at you to go and do something proper for a living, it seems so unrealistic that you will ever work as an actor.

But if it's what you want to do, you have to fight and fight and fight, and carry on fighting.

Mark Umbers

Acknowledgements

Huge thanks are due to all the actors who kindly gave up their time to talk me through the pleasures and pitfalls of their profession – at length, and often on their lunch breaks from the rehearsal room, or while stealing a moment alone in their on-set trailers. I'm very grateful also to their agents, publicists and assistants for sharing my enthusiasm for this project.

Thanks to Matt Applewhite, my lovely editor at Nick Hern Books, for his guidance and insight. Thanks to JB and IB, for giving me a love of theatre that I have never lost, and the respect for actors that goes hand in hand with it. And thanks, above all, to the actor I married, for showing me what it is to live that crazy, maddening, wonderful life.

L.B.